The Framework of the Chinese Government and Public Services

Jiang Haishan, Jiang Junjie, Yu Hongsheng

Published by
ACA Publishing Ltd.
University House
11-13 Lower Grosvenor Place,
London SW1W 0EX, UK
Tel: +44 (0)20 7834 7676 Fax: +44 (0)20 7973 0076
E-mail: info@alaincharlesasia.com

Web: www.alaincharlesasia.com
Beijing Office
Tel:+86(0)10 8472 1250 Fax:86(0)10 5885 0639
Written by Jiang Haishan, Jiang Junjie, Yu Hongsheng
Edited by David Lammie, ACA Publishing Ltd
© People's Publishing House, 2015
This translation is published by ACA Publishing Ltd in association with People's Publishing House

ALL RIGHTS RESERVED. NO PART OF THIS
PUBLICATION MAY BE REPRODUCED IN MATERIAL FORM,
BY ANY MEANS, WHETHER GRAPHIC,
ELECTRONIC, MECHANICAL OR OTHER, INCLUDING
PHOTOCOPYING OR INFORMATION STORAGE, IN
WHOLE OR IN PART, AND MAY NOT BE USED TO PREPARE
OTHER PUBLICATIONS WITHOUT WRITTEN
PERMISSION FROM THE PUBLISHER.

The greatest care has been taken to ensure accuracy but the publisher can accept no responsibility for errors or omissions, or for any liability occasioned by relying on its content.
ISBN 978-1-910760-13-0
The Framework of the Chinese Government and Public Services is available from the National Bibliographic Service of the British Library.

Preface

What is the state system of China? How has the Communist Party of China (CPC) managed to exercize long-term governance and to lead the Chinese people from one victory to another? What are the 'secrets' of the CPC's governance? What is China's development road? What significant strategies have been adopted in China? What is the next step in China's development? Why has China been able to achieve such rapid economic development? These are just some of the many questions frequently asked by the international community, especially foreign political parties and statesmen on their visits to China. For the purpose of providing answers to these questions and enabling readers to be informed about the real China and the CPC, we arranged for the *Understanding Modern China* Series (hereinafter referred to as the Series) to be written, to serve as elementary documents introducing the CPC, as well as China's development road, development theories and development experience.

The Series has been written on the basis of telling China's story and transmitting China's voice, oriented around the following four aspects: the first is to illustrate the new measures taken to deepen reform since the 18th National Congress of the CPC, the new ideas on economic development and the new philosophy on foreign affairs, on the basis of an all-round introduction to the achievements since the reform and opening up; the second is to analyze the reason for the achievements, the underlying operating law, and the process of evolution, while presenting the development achievements of China's economy and society; the third is to keep to problem orientation and demand orientation, rather than attempt to be all-embracing and systematic, so as to clear up targeted doubts and confusion on the basis of the demands of foreign readers; the fourth is to introduce China not only in terms of 'where it comes from', but also in terms of 'where it is going', for the purpose of enabling readers to know about China's historical development process on the one hand, and on the other hand, exemplifying and clarifying how China assures the organic unification of its past, present and future, the organic combination of inheritance and innovation, and how China is planning its future development.

Under the guidance of the International Department of the CPC Central Committee, the writing of the Series has been organized by China Executive Leadership Academy Pudong (CELAP).

The International Department of the CPC Central Committee is the functional department of the CPC in charge of foreign affairs. So far the CPC has established connections of various types with more than 600 political parties and organizations in over 160 countries and regions, which include left-wing and right-wing parties; both ruling parties and opposition parties. Foreign affairs work is of paramount importance to the CPC, and an indispensable component of national diplomacy as a whole, whose target is to promote state-to-state and people-to-people communication and understanding.

CELAP is a national leadership institution in China, and as a platform on which international cooperative training and exchange are carried out, CELAP has held fast to its characteristics of internationality and openness since March 2005 when it was founded. CELAP spares no effort to implement international cooperative training, with target participants being foreign political parties and statesmen, high-ranking business executives and senior professionals. By the end of 2015, CELAP had offered training programs to more than 6,000 participants from over 130 countries, and thus has won wide recognition and received a favorable reception from the countries, regions and participants that are involved.

To cater for the needs of foreign participants, CELAP initiated the writing of the Series at the beginning of 2012, and after four years of modifications and improvements, the finalized manuscripts were completed at the end of 2015. The first batch of 10 books to be published in this Series cover: *China's New Strategy for Governing the Country; The CPC: A History of Party Building, 1921-2015; A Concise History of China's Reform, Opening Up and Development Zones; An Insider's Guide to the Inner Workings and Structure of the Chinese Government And Public Services; A Concise History of Urbanization in China; China's Agriculture and Rural Development in the Post-reform Era; The Evolution of China's Diplomacy in the Modern Era; The Selection and Appointment of Officials in China; The Education and Training*

Preface

of Officials in China; and *Shanghai - the 'Pacesetter' of China's Reform and Opening Up.*

The authors of the Series are mainly professionals in CELAP, and functionaries and specialists in the Development Research Center of the Shanghai Municipal People's Government, Shanghai Institute for International Studies, and Hangzhou Research Center for Urban Studies.

The Series is published in Chinese and English, with the English translation done mainly by senior professors at Shanghai International Studies University, to whom thanks are due. Gratitude also goes to the People's Publishing House for its great support and positive suggestions in the process of writing and translating.

Writing such a series of textbooks for foreign learners is a first in China. Constructive criticism is welcome, for the Series as a new endeavor can hardly be free from mistakes.

Editorial Committee of the *Understanding Modern China* Series

January 2016

The Editorial Committee of the Understanding Modern China Series

Director: Guo Yezhou Feng Jun
Vice Director: Zhou Zhongfei An Yuejun
Members: (Listed alphabetically)

An Yuejun	Chen Zhong	
Feng Jun	Guo Yezhou	
He Lisheng	Jiang Haishan	Liu Genfa
Liu Jingbei	Li Man	Li Yanhui
Wang Guoping	Wang Jinding	Yang Jiemian
Zheng Jinzhou	Zhao Shiming	Zhou Zhongfei
Zhou Zhenhua		

Editor-in-Chief: Feng Jun

Alain Charles Asia (ACA) Publishing Ltd is delighted to be associated with the People's Publishing House to bring this series of 10 *Understanding Modern China* books to an English-speaking readership.

ACA, formerly known as ACP (Alain Charles Publishing) Ltd Beijing, was founded in October 1989 and was the first foreign-owned publishing company to be allowed to open an office in China.

In 2007, ACP Beijing was renamed ACA Publishing Ltd to better reflect its focus on China and the Asia-Pacific region. The company specialises in publishing books about China for international readers and has offices in Beijing and London.

ACA Publishing Ltd,

April 2016

Contents

Introduction IX
    I. Objectives IX
    II. Structure of the Book IX
    III. Focuses and Difficulties XI
    IV. Some Advice XII

1. China's Political System 1
    I. National People's Congress 1
    II. System of Multi-party Cooperation and Political Consultation under the Leadership of the CPC 7
    III. China's Regional Ethnic Autonomy System 13
    IV. China's System of Mass Self-government at the Grassroots Level 15

2. China's Governments 22
    I. Composition and Powers of the State Council 22
    II. China's Administrative Divisions, Local State Organs and their Functions 28

3. China's Public Services System Reform 36
    I. Implications of China's Household Registration System on Public Services 36
    II. Measures Taken by the Chinese Government to Promote the Equalization of Basic Public Services 41

4. China's Education Reform 47
    I. Evolution of China's Education Strategy 47
    II. Main Achievements of CE in China 48
    III. Major Obstacles and Countermeasures in Promoting Equal Access to CE in China 50

5. China's Public Employment Service Reform 56

  I. PES System in China 56
  II. Key Services Provided by the PES System in China 57
  III. Systems, Mechanisms and Policies adopted by the Chinese Government to Improve the PES System 63

6. China's Health Care System Reform 71
  I. Basic Facts and Figures about China's Health Care System 71
  II. China's Medical and Health Care System Reform 73
  III. Measures Taken by the Chinese Government to Ensure Universal Access to Basic Health Care Services 78
  IV. International Health Care Cooperation by the Chinese Government ..84

7. China's Basic Elderly Care Reform 86
  I. Basic Elderly Care in China 86
  II. Family-supported Elderly Care System in China 88
  III. Modern Social Elderly Care Model in China 89
  IV. Measures to Improve the Rural Elderly Care Insurance System 91
  V. Elderly Care Challenges that an Ageing China Faces 93
  VI. Measures to Build a Fairer and More Sustainable Social Security System in China 95

8. China's Reform of the Housing Security and Social Relief Systems 103
  I. China's Multi-level Housing Security System 103
  II. China's Social Relief System 107
  III. China's Poverty-alleviation Policy 115

Chapter Follow-up Questions and References 118

Introduction

I. Objectives

This textbook aims to introduce the framework of the Chinese government and its public services. It introduces China's constitution and the operation of the National People's Congress (NPC), the Chinese People's Political Consultative Conference (CPPCC), the central people's government and local governments. Emphasis is put on analyzing the reforms in China's public service sector, its current state and policies, such as the equalization of public services. It also discusses the current situation, transformation and prospective development of governmental policies on free education, employment, medical care, welfare for senior citizens and residents, and relief policies. This textbook adopts a people-oriented approach and underscores fairness and justice. The authors wish to demonstrate the innovation and best practices of the Chinese government in the transformation of government practice as well as public welfare.

II. Structure of the Book

There are eight chapters in this book. The first chapter introduces the structure and operation process of China's political system. Most important and first of all, China's fundamental political system is the people's congress system. This chapter focuses on analyzing the elections of representatives to the NPC, the main functions of the NPC, the rights and authorities of the NPC Standing Committee, and the functions of NPC special committees.

Second, the system of multi-party cooperation and political consultation under the leadership of the Communist Party of China (CPC) is another basic political system in China. The structure and operation of the Central Committee of the CPC, the role of the Chinese people's united patriotic front, the Chinese People's Political Consultative Conference, and its role of political consultation, democratic supervision and participation in the deliberation and administration of state affairs are also introduced.

The first chapter goes on to discuss the system of regional ethnic autonomy in China, analyzes the composition and operation of the system as well as the autonomy of the local organs of autonomous governments. The system of grassroots mass autonomy in China, covering both rural and urban areas, is also presented.

The second chapter analyzes the structure and operation process of the Chinese government. It begins by introducing the nature, functions and powers of the State Council and continues with an introduction to China's administrative division, local governments and the powers, main functions, and operating process of the constitution. It also sheds lights on China's implementation of the policy of 'one country, two systems', which is of great significance, the meaning of special administrative regions and their powers.

The third chapter focuses on the reform of China's public service system, and the policy of providing equal access to public services. It analyzes the historical evolution of China's household registration system, its reform, and the strategic significance to abolish the double-track urban and rural registration. Then, this chapter analyzes the measures to promote equal access to public services in order to narrow the gap between urban and rural areas and among different regions. The reform of the public finance system is also covered.

The fourth chapter introduces the education system in China, its strategic planning, and the major achievements after the 'two basics' goal was achieved. It highlights the policy of providing nine years of free and compulsory education in rural and urban areas, and ends with an analysis on the major problems and policies in promoting compulsory education in China.

The fifth chapter introduces the public employment service system in China and its reforms. The basic role and policy framework of the public employment service system is discussed. It goes on to introduce the main methods of promoting public employment services in China, including employment assistance, public training, business services, government procurement and employment services. This chapter also introduces the mechanism of the Chinese government's efforts in promoting employment and entrepreneurship.

Introduction

Chapter six focuses on reforms in China's medical and health care system. It analyzes the evolution of health care reforms, and points out the distinctive historical features of the health care system after taking a close look at its evolution. This chapter also assesses the measures that the Chinese government takes to ensure that everyone has access to basic health care, including the establishment of a national supply system of essential drugs, and the improvements made to the medical security system. International cooperation in this field is also introduced.

Chapter seven covers basic old-age security reform in China. Based on an analysis of the history of China's basic old-age security system, this chapter focuses on family pensions and China's modern social security system. It also introduces measures to improve the rural pension insurance system in China. It goes on to look at the challenges posed by an ageing population in China. It also points out the measures taken by the Chinese government in constructing a more equitable and sustainable social security system.

The eighth chapter focuses on analyzing China's housing security system as well as the reform of the social relief system. This chapter introduces China's housing fund system, along with systems addressing affordable housing, low rent housing and public rental housing. It also analyzes the social relief system, which includes an urban residents' relief system, minimum living wage system for rural residents, medical assistance system, and system for providing assistance to people who beg on the streets. The chapter ends by providing an overview of China's poverty-alleviation policy. It discusses the distinctive historical features and how the policies evolve.

III. Focuses and Difficulties

This textbook focuses on introducing the basic framework and operation process of the Chinese government, the reform and development of public service in China, and recent reform initiatives. The purpose is to help students understand how China's government management system operates based on its people-oriented principles, how it is reforming and adopting innovative measures to provide public service, how it gradually realizes the basic rights of Chinese citizens in terms of education, employment, medical care, pensions, housing, social relief and so on, and how it achieves the ultimate goal of social justice. Students should pay special attention to making sure that they understand how China's current situation has determined its political system, the complex relationship among the CPC, the People's Congress and the people's government. This book also underscores the inner logic of China's public service system reform, in which the government used to take care of everything, but now it strives to manage the different needs of diversified participants.

IV. Some Advice

Students are expected to read this textbook and compare what they learn with the experience of other countries. Some basic knowledge and concepts of government are required. In order to better appreciate the contents, students are advised to take a comparative and international approach, and to make objective comments after considering the history, culture and other specifics of China. The authors aim to provide a vivid description of the evolution of China's public service system, hoping that students can appreciate recent developments and obstacles to reform. Students are also advised to look at the governmental systems of China from a broader comparative perspective.

This textbook naturally has its limitations. We hope that those who make use of it are willing to share their valuable opinions. This textbook is written under the constant guidance of Jiang Haishan, vice president of China Executive Leadership Academy Pudong. Authors of individual chapters are: Jiang Junjie (Introduction, 1, 2, 3), Yu Hongsheng, Li Siling, Jiang Junjie (3), Wen Wenyan, Ding Jinfeng (4), Wu Jinbao (5), Zhou Yi (6), Liu Genfa (7) and Li De (8). Under the supervision of Professor Yu Hongsheng, Jiang Junjie reviewed the whole book. We welcome any constructive criticism on any part of the book that might be flawed.

Chapter 1

China's Political System

This section describes how the Chinese political system has been operating since October 1, 1949, the founding of the PRC. The system of state power, government, and national and social structure are introduced. A series of fundamental issues, including laws, systems, rules and practices are discussed in general. It gives an overview of China's people's congress system, regional autonomy system and the multi-party cooperation and political consultation system under the leadership of the CPC, as well as the grassroots mass autonomy system.

I. National People's Congress

The NPC is the supreme organ of state power in China. Its Standing Committee is the permanent body of the NPC and both exercise legislative power at the national level.

1. Election of deputies to the National People's Congress

Deputies to the NPC are elected according to law. Laws stipulate that any citizen of the PRC, regardless of nationality, race, sex, occupation, family background, religious belief, education, property status or length of residence, has the right to vote and to be elected, unless he/she has been deprived of political rights in accordance with the law.

As specified in the *Electoral Law of the PRC (2010)*, people's congresses that are below county level have their deputies directly elected by the voters; deputies to the people's congress at or above the county level are elected by people's congresses at lower levels that are directly under their jurisdiction. Deputies to the NPC are elected from province-level congresses, congresses of autonomous regions and of municipalities directly under the jurisdiction of the central government; deputies from the People's Liberation Army (PLA) are elected separately.

According to the *Electoral Law (2010)*, deputies to the NPC are voted by secret ballot; the number of candidates for deputies to be elected by various local people's congresses to the people's congresses at the next higher level shall be 20-50% greater than the number of deputies to be elected. Political parties and people's organizations may either jointly or separately recommend candidates for deputies. A joint group of at least 10 voters or deputies may also recommend candidates. Where a local people's congress at or above county level is to elect deputies to the people's congress at the next higher level, the election shall be presided over by the presidium of the lower people's congress.

There should be no more than 3,000 deputies to the NPC. Quotas should be allocated by the Standing Committee of the NPC depending on specific situations. The number of deputies elected from Hong Kong and Macau special administrative regions (SARs) to the NPC, as well as their elections, shall be stipulated separately by the NPC.

In an election, candidates for deputies shall be elected only if they have obtained more than half of the votes of all the deputies. When the number of candidates for deputies who have obtained more than half of the votes exceeds the number of deputies to be elected, those who have obtained the most votes shall be elected. If the number of votes for some candidates is tied, making it impossible to determine who is elected, another ballot shall be conducted between those candidates to resolve the tie. The presidium of the People's Congress shall decide whether the outcome is valid and announce the outcome. Election funds for the NPC and local people's congresses at various levels shall be disbursed by the State Treasury. Elections are chaired by the Standing Committee of the NPC.

The number of deputies to the NPC on behalf of the provinces, autonomous regions and municipalities directly under the central government shall be distributed by the Standing Committee of the NPC in accordance with the principle that each generation should have the same number of representatives.

The number of deputies to the NPC to be elected by minority nationalities shall be allocated by the Standing Committee of the NPC, in light of the population and distribution of each minority nationality, to the people's congresses of the various provinces, autonomous regions and municipalities directly under the central government, which shall elect them accordingly. Nationalities with exceptionally small populations shall each have at least one deputy. The *Electoral Law (2010)* also stipulates that, among deputies to the NPC and local people's congresses at various levels, there shall be an appropriate number of women deputies, and that their proportion should increase gradually. Furthermore, there shall be an appropriate number of returned overseas Chinese.

2. Legal provisions on the election of ethnic minorities

The 18th clause of the *Electoral Law (2010)* stipulates that, in areas where minority nationalities live in concentrated communities, each minority nationality shall have its deputy or deputies sit in the local people's congress.

Where the total population of a minority nationality in such an area exceeds 30% of the total local population, the number of people represented by each deputy of that minority nationality shall be equal to the number of people represented by each of the other deputies to the local people's congress.

Where the total population of a minority nationality in such an area is less than 15% of the total local population, the number of people represented by each deputy of that minority nationality may be appropriately smaller, but shall not be less than half the number of people represented by each of the other deputies to the local people's congress. In autonomous counties where the population of the minority nationality practicing regional autonomy is exceptionally small, the number of people represented by each deputy of this minority nationality may, upon a decision made by the standing committee of the people's congress of the province or autonomous region, be fewer than half the number of people represented by each of the other deputies. Other nationalities with exceptionally small populations living in concentrated communities shall each have at least one deputy.

Where the total population of a minority nationality in such an area accounts for not less than 15% and not more than 30% of the total local population, the number of people represented by each deputy of that minority nationality may be appropriately smaller than the number of people represented by each of the other deputies to the local people's congress, but the allocated number of deputies to be elected by that minority nationality shall not exceed 30% of the total number of deputies.

3. Main functions and powers of the NPC

The NPC is the supreme organ of state power. According to the provisions of the constitution, the NPC has full and the highest authority. Its main functions are:

(1) To amend the constitution and to supervise its enforcement

The constitution is the fundamental law of the state; it has the highest legal authority. Only the NPC has the power to amend the constitution. It would require a two-thirds majority vote for the constitution to be revised, whether it is a comprehensive revision or a revision of specific clauses. No other authority, political party or organization has such a jurisdiction.

(2) To enact and amend the fundamental laws of the state

The constitution stipulates that the NPC shall enact and amend basic laws governing criminal offences, civil affairs, the state organs and other matters.

(3) To elect, appoint or remove personnel of national institutions

According to the constitution and law, the NPC has the power to elect and remove members, the secretary general, vice-chairman and chairman of the Standing Committee of the NPC. It shall elect and remove the president and vice-president of the PRC. It decides on the choice of the premier of the State Council upon nomination by the president of the PRC, and on the choice of the vice-premiers, state councilors, ministers in charge of ministries or commissions, the auditor general and the secretary general of the State Council upon nomination by the premier. It elects the chairman of the Central Military Commission (CMC) and, upon nomination by the chairman, decides on the choice of all other members of the commission. It also elects and removes the president of the Supreme People's Court and the procurator general of the Supreme People's Procuratorate. It appoints members, deputy directors and directors of special committees of the NPC. The NPC has the power to remove from office any of the above-mentioned officials.

(4) To determine major state issues

This work includes examining and approving the report on the plan for national economic and social development and on its implementation; examining and approving the report on the central and local budgets and their implementation; approving the establishment of provinces, autonomous regions and municipalities directly under the jurisdiction of the State Council; deciding where to establish special administrative regions and what system they should institute; deciding on questions of war and peace; and granting authorization.

(5) To supervise state organs

The NPC has the highest authority of supervision. The constitution provides that: (a) the Standing Committee of the NPC is responsible to and reports to the NPC; (b) the administrative, judicial and procuratorial organs of the state are produced by, and report to, the people's congresses; (c) the chairman of the CMC reports to the NPC. The NPC is also responsible for supervising the CMC. According to the provisions of the constitution and laws, the major approach of supervision is to hear and review the reports of the Standing Committee of the NPC, the State Council, the Supreme People's Court and the Supreme People's Procuratorate.

4. Powers of the standing committee of the NPC

The Standing Committee is a permanent body of the NPC. According to the constitution and the law on the organization of the NPC, the powers and authorities of the Standing Committee shall include:

(1) Legislative power

According to the provisions of the current constitution, the Standing Committee and the NPC shall jointly exercise legislative power. These legislative powers mainly include: the drafting and revision of laws except those that shall be enacted by the NPC; when the NPC is not in session, to partially supplement and amend laws enacted by the NPC provided that the basic principles of these laws are not contravened.

(2) Right to interpret the constitution and laws

To interpret the constitution is to further clarify the boundaries or make supplementary provisions to the law. This is designed to ensure that problems raised during the enforcement of the constitution and laws shall be answered, and therefore to ensure accuracy in law enforcement.

(3) Rights to supervise the enforcement of the constitution

The current constitution gives authority both to the NPC and its Standing Committee to supervise the enforcement of the constitution. As a permanent body, the Standing Committee is better positioned to ensure regular supervision, which is of great significance to the successful enforcement of the constitution.

(4) Rights to supervise the work of other state organs

The Standing Committee supervises the work of the State Council, the CMC, the Supreme People's Court and the Supreme People's Procuratorate. It has the power to annul those administrative rules and regulations, decisions or orders of the State Council that contravene the constitution or the law, and those local regulations or decisions of the organs of state power of provinces, autonomous regions and municipalities directly under the jurisdiction of the State Council that contravene the constitution, the law or administrative rules and regulations.

(5) Rights to appoint and remove other state personnel

(a) To decide, when the NPC is not in session, on the choice of ministers in charge of ministries or commissions, the auditor-general or the secretary-general of the State Council upon nomination by the premier of the State Council; (b) to decide, upon nomination by the chairman of the CMC, on the choice of other members of the commission, when the NPC is not in session; (c) to appoint or remove, at the recommendation of the president of the Supreme People's Court, the vice-presidents and Judges of the Supreme People's Court, members of its Judicial Committee and the president of the Military Court; (d) to appoint or remove, at the recommendation of the procurator general of the Supreme People's Procuratorate, the deputy procurators general and procurators of the Supreme People's Procuratorate, members of its procuratorial committee and the chief procurator of the Military Procuratorate, and to approve the appointment or removal of the chief procurators of the people's procuratorates of provinces, autonomous regions and municipalities directly under the jurisdiction of the State Council; (e) to decide on the appointment or recall of plenipotentiary representatives abroad.

(6) Rights to decide on important state affairs

This authority includes: (a) to decide on the ratification or abrogation of treaties and important agreements concluded with foreign states; (b) to institute systems of titles and ranks for military and diplomatic personnel and of other specific titles and ranks; (c) to institute state medals and titles of honor and decide on their conferment; (d) to decide on the granting of special pardons; (e) to decide, when the NPC is not in session, on the proclamation of a state of war in the event of an armed attack on the country or in fulfillment of international treaty obligations concerning common defense against aggression; (f) to decide on general mobilization or partial mobilization; (g) to decide on the imposition of martial law throughout the country or in particular provinces, autonomous regions or municipalities directly under the jurisdiction of the State Council; (h) to review and approve, when the NPC is not in session, partial adjustments to the plan for national economic and social development or to the state budget that prove necessary in the course of their implementation.

(7) Other powers conferred by the NPC

In addition to the aforementioned functions, the NPC Standing Committee has the right to exercise other functions and powers such as the NPC may assign to it, including: (a) chairing the election of deputies to the NPC; (b) convening a session of the NPC; (c) contacting deputies of the NPC, and organizing them to an inspection mission; (d) when the NPC is not in session, leading the work of the special committee.

5. Special committees of the NPC

The NPC establishes a Nationalities Committee, a Law Committee, a Finance and Economic Committee, an Education, Science, Culture and Public Health Committee, a Foreign Affairs Committee, an Overseas Chinese Committee, a Civil Affairs and Judiciary Committee, an Environment and Resource Protection Committee, an Agriculture and Rural Area Committee and other special committees as are necessary. These special committees work under the direction of the Standing Committee of the NPC when the congress is not in session. The special committees examine, discuss and draw up relevant bills and draft resolutions under the direction of the NPC and its Standing Committee. The NPC and its Standing Committee may, when they deem it necessary, appoint committees of inquiry into specific questions and adopt relevant resolutions in the light of their reports.

II. System of Multi-party Cooperation and Political Consultation under the Leadership of the CPC

1. Central organization of the CPC

According to the constitution of the CPC, the party's central organizations include: the National Congress of the Party and its Central Committee, the Central Commission for Discipline Inspection, the Central Political Bureau, the Standing Committee of the Central Political Bureau, the Secretariat of the Central Committee and the Military Commission of the Central Committee. The constitution further stipulates that the national congress of the party is held once every five years and convened by the Central Committee. It may be convened before the normally scheduled date if the Central Committee deems it necessary or if requested by more than one-third of the organizations at provincial level. Except under extraordinary circumstances, the congress may not be postponed.

The functions and powers of the National Congress of the party are as follows: (1) to hear and examine the reports of the Central Committee; (2) to hear and examine the reports of the Central Commission for Discipline Inspection; (3) to discuss and decide on major questions concerning the party; (4) to revise the constitution of the party; (5) to elect the Central Committee; and (6) to elect the Central Commission for Discipline Inspection.

The Central Committee of the party is elected for a term of five years. However, when the next National Congress is convened before or after its normally scheduled date, the term shall be correspondingly shortened or extended. Members and alternate members of the Central Committee must be in the party for no less than five years. The Central Committee of the Party meets in plenary session at least once a year, and such sessions are convened by its Political Bureau. When the National Congress is not in session, the Central Committee carries out its resolutions, directs the entire work of the party and represents the CPC in its external relations.

The Political Bureau, the Standing Committee of the Political Bureau and the general secretary of the Central Committee of the Party are elected by the Central Committee in plenary session. The general secretary of the Central Committee must be a member of the Standing Committee of the Political Bureau. When the Central Committee is not in session, the Political Bureau and its Standing Committee exercise the functions and powers of the Central Committee. The Secretariat of the Central Committee is the working body of the Political Bureau of the Central Committee and its Standing Committee. The members of the Secretariat are nominated by the Standing Committee of the Political Bureau of the Central Committee and are subject to endorsement by the Central Committee in plenary session. The general secretary of the Central Committee is responsible for convening the meetings of the Political Bureau and its Standing Committee and presides over the work of the secretariat. The members of the Military Commission of the Central Committee are decided on by the Central Committee. The central leading bodies and leaders elected by each Central Committee shall, when the next National Congress is in session, continue to preside over the party's day-to-day work until the new central leading bodies and leaders are elected by the next Central Committee.

The party organization of the PLA carry on their work in accordance with the instructions of the Central Committee. The political work of the CMC is the PLA's General Political Department; the General Political Department is responsible for the management of the army in the party's work and political work. The party's organization system and organization in the army shall make provisions for the CMC.

Structural Chart of the CPC

National Congress
- Central Committee
  - Central Secretary of the Central Committee
  - Standing Committee of the Central Politburo
  - Central Politburo
  - Central Secretariat
  - Central Military Commission
- Central Commission for Discipline Inspection

2. Political consultative conference

The Chinese People's Political Consultative Conference (CPPCC) is the organization of the Chinese people's patriotic united front, an important institution under the multi-party cooperation and political consultation system under the leadership of the CPC, and an important player in China's political life that embodies socialist democracy. The CPPCC gives political consultation on important issues concerning national policies and people's livelihoods, and it plays an important role of participation through giving suggestions and criticisms and in the deliberation and administration of state affairs. It is also an important means of democratic supervision.

(1) The main work of the CPPCC is political consultation

Political consultation is the consultation before making a decision on important questions concerning national and local policies, political, economic, cultural and social issues, and while the decision is being carried out. The CPPCC is a crucial part of the multi-party cooperation and political consultation system under the leadership of the CPC. Democratic supervision is another major work. It supervises the enforcement of the constitution, laws and regulations of the state, the implementation of major policies, state organs and their staff work by giving suggestions and criticisms. It means that, not only members of the CPPCC, including those from political parties, people's organizations and all walks of life, supervise the work of the state organs and their staff members, but also members from the CPC and other political parties supervise each others' work under this framework. Political participation is another essential function. Members of the conference carry out research and interviews regarding major issues in the country's political, economic, cultural and social life, organize consultations and discussions to represent citizens' opinions, and submit suggestions to the CPC and all kinds of state organs. They may submit investigation reports, proposals, recommendations and other documents.

(2) The composition and operation of the CPPCC

According to the Charter of the CPPCC adopted in 1982, the conference is divided into the national committee and local committees. The National Committee of the CPPCC shall be composed of the CPC, the various democratic parties, public personages without party affiliation, people's organizations, ethnic minority groups and people from all walks of life, compatriots of Hong Kong special administrative region (SAR), Macau SAR and Taiwan, returned overseas Chinese and specially invited personalities. The term of each national committee of the CPPCC shall be five years. The National Committee of the CPPCC shall have one chairman and a number of vice-chairmen and a secretary general.

Political parties in the conference include: the CPC, the Revolutionary Committee of the Chinese Kuomintang, China Democratic League, Organization on Democratic Establishment of China, the China Association for the Promotion of Democracy, the Chinese Peasants' and Workers' Democratic Party, China Zhi Gong Dang, the Jiusan Society and the Taiwan Democratic Self-government League.

The National Committee shall hold a plenary session every year. It shall exercise its functions as follows: 1. making amendments to the charter of the CPPCC and supervising their implementation; 2. electing the chairman, vice-chairmen, secretary general and members of the Standing Committee; 3. hearing and examining work reports of the Standing Committee; 4. deliberating on and making resolutions on major work principles and tasks; 5. and participating in the discussion of major state policies and advancing proposals and criticisms.

Standing Committee The Standing Committee of the CPPCC National Committee shall be composed of the chairman, vice-chairmen, secretary general and standing committee members, to be elected by the plenary session of the National Committee from among the candidates proposed by the political parties, organizations, nationalities and personages from all walks of life participating in the CPPCC National Committee. The Chairman of the CPPCC National Committee presides over the work of the Standing Committee, with assistance from the vice-chairmen and secretary general. The chairman, vice-chairmen and secretary general make up the chairmen's meetings and take care of major day-to-day affairs. The CPPCC National Committee shall establish a number of special committees and other working institutions to meet the needs of work.

Special committees Special committees are working bodies that organize members of the CPPCC to carry out their work. They operate under the leadership of the Standing Committee and the chairmen's meetings. Each special committee shall have one director, several deputy directors and members.

Local committees Provinces, autonomous regions, municipalities under the direct jurisdiction of the State Council, autonomous prefectures, counties, autonomous counties, cities and municipal districts all have CPPCC organizations wherever possible. To date, there have been more than 3,000 local CPPCC committees, and a total of some 500,000 local CPPCC members.

CPPCC members CPPCC members are appointed by recommendation. The list of elected members shall be determined by the Standing Committee with permission from the chairman's meetings of the previous CPPCC national committee. CPPCC members are representative and socially influential from all fields and walks of life in China.

(3) **The appointments of members**

CPPCC members are appointed by recommendation through consultation. The number of members and candidates should be decided by the Standing Committee after consultation with the chairman's meetings of the previous session. CPPCC members are representative and socially influential from all fields and walks of life in China and are capable of political participation. The minimum age requirement is 18, and traditionally only citizens of the PRC can be appointed, though technically overseas Chinese and people who are currently citizens of Taiwan area can also participate.

(4) **The main approaches**

Meetings Meetings are the main form by which the CPPCC performs its functions. The main meeting systems of the National Committee include: a general assembly, meeting of the Standing Committee, chairman's meeting, meeting of secretary general and meeting of the special committees. In addition, whenever necessary, other forms of meeting include consultative forums, hearings and opinion polls.

Proposals Proposals refer to the written recommendations and comments submitted by CPPCC members, political parties participating in the CPPCC, and special committees of the CPPCC to the plenary session of the CPPCC or the Standing Committee. After being reviewed, they are sent to responsible authorities for implementation. The proposals are generally put forward in four ways: first, CPPCC members can extend a personal or a joint proposal; second, when the plenary meeting is in session, members can submit proposals in their field or fields. Third, political parties and people's organizations can bring forward proposals in their own names or do so jointly. Fourth, the special committees can propose in their own names, or jointly. Responsible authorities should carry out related proposals according to relevant regulations and send a written reply before the deadline. The National Committee takes supervision in a variety of ways.

Inspection Inspection is the foundation for CPPCC members to perform their duties; it is an important way through which members shall understand situations, review work, research problems and put forward proposals; it is an important channel by which members carry out their democratic rights and supervise. The National Committee organizes inspections every year according to national priorities.

Research The CPPCC also carries out research projects and brings forward suggestions. This is an important way by which the CPPCC makes use of its advantage and helps in matters of the nation. In order to conduct this research, the CPPCC usually commission special committees and requires the committees to invite scholars and experts from all fields to give their ideas on the most important work of the nation and, after discussion, put forward practical comments and suggestions. In this way, the CPPCC contributes a great deal to the coordinated development of the nations' economy, democracy and culture.

Reflections on social conditions and public opinion Understanding and reporting social situations and public opinion is an important basis and key procedure of the CPPCC to perform its functions. CPPCC members are required to maintain close contact with the mass public so they can report what is going on and consider it in a timely, comprehensive manner. This will help the government to understand current affairs and therefore make sensible decisions, and also help to solve practical issues.

Promoting the reunification of China The CPPCC has been adamantly carrying out policies of 'peaceful reunification and one country, two systems'; it aims to strengthen contact with the relevant authorities, expanding the channels of contact with people from all walks of life in Hong Kong, Macau and Taiwan. It organizes various activities in an effort to unite compatriots in Hong Kong, Macau, Taiwan area and overseas Chinese for the full reunification of our motherland.

Encouraging foreign exchange The activities of the CPPCC form an important part of China's overall diplomatic effort. Its foreign exchanges are based on the overall needs of the nation's diplomacy. The CPPCC is committed to strengthening friendly exchanges and cooperation with other countries, and to safeguarding world peace and promote common development.

III. China's Regional Ethnic Autonomy System

1. Basic introduction to the system of regional ethnic autonomy in China

The system of regional ethnic autonomy means that, where minorities live in compact communities, organs of self-government are established under the unified leadership of the state. Minority peoples exercise autonomous rights, are masters in their own areas and administer their own internal affairs. The practice of a regional ethnic autonomy system is chosen based on China's history, cultural specifics, relations among ethnic groups and the distribution of ethnic minorities.

Autonomous organs are divided into three levels: autonomous regions, autonomous prefectures and autonomous counties. At present, China has established 155 autonomous areas, comprising five autonomous regions, 30 autonomous prefectures and 120 autonomous counties. Of the 55 ethnic minorities groups, 44 have been their own autonomous areas, and 71% of the total population of minority nationalities live in autonomous areas.

2. The autonomous powers of autonomous organs

(1) Ethnic legislative power

The people's congresses in autonomous areas shall, in accordance with the particularities of local political, economic and cultural life, draft autonomous regulations and separate regulations. The autonomous regulations stipulate the basic issues concerning regional ethnic autonomy, while the separate regulations are provisions regarding specific matters relating to the implementation of ethnic autonomy in a certain area. Autonomous regulations and separate regulations can make flexible alterations to existing laws, administrative regulations or local laws of the state. They shall be submitted to the Standing Committee of the NPC for approval. The autonomous regulations and separate regulations of autonomous prefectures and counties shall be submitted to the Standing Committee of the provincial or autonomous region level people's congress for approval, and then the Standing Committee of the NPC must be informed.

(2) Rights of flexibility

If the resolutions, decisions, orders and directives of state organs at higher levels are not suitable for the particular situation of an autonomous area, the organs of self-government may report the matter to the higher state organs concerned, asking for permission to flexibly carry out, or halt the carrying out, of those resolutions, decisions, orders and directives.

(3) Fiscal and economic autonomy

The organs of self-government of national autonomous areas shall have a greater degree of fiscal and economic autonomy, and can enjoy the care and preferential treatment of the state. As long as those incomes, according to state regulations, belong to autonomous organ, it shall have the autonomy to allocate those funds. The State Council gives preferential policies regarding budgeting and spending in autonomous areas. Autonomous areas can put in place an emergency fund, which in accordance with state regulations, enjoys a higher proportion in the area's budget.

(4) Using and developing the spoken and written languages of ethnic groups

According to the provisions of the self-government regulations for ethnic autonomous areas, the organs of self-government of such areas shall use one or more commonly used local languages when they perform official duties. If more than one language can be used for such official duties, the language of the ethnic group exercising regional autonomy should be used primarily.

(5) The right to organize public security forces

The organs of self-government of national autonomous areas may, in accordance with the military system of the state and practical local needs, and with the approval of the State Council, organize local public security forces for the maintenance of public order.

(6) Functionaries of ethnic minority groups enjoy priority in promotion

In all of China's 155 national autonomous areas, the chairman or vice-chairman of the Standing Committee of the local People's Congress is a member of the ethnic group exercising regional autonomy. The chairman of an autonomous region, the prefect of an autonomous prefecture or the head of an autonomous county shall be a citizen of the nationality exercising regional autonomy in that area. Other posts in the people's government of an autonomous region, autonomous prefecture or autonomous county should, whenever possible, be assumed by people of the nationality exercising regional autonomy and of other minority nationalities in the area concerned, in accordance with the law.

IV. China's System of Mass Self-government at the Grassroots Level

The system of mass self-government at the grassroots level is one that, under the framework of the constitution of the PRC, led by grassroots organizations of the CPC, through grassroots-level mass self-government organizations, allow people to exercise their political rights in a direct way and achieve self management, self service, self education and self supervision. Article 111 of the constitution of the PRC (1982) stipulates that residents' committees and villagers' committees established among urban and rural residents on the basis of their place of residence are mass organizations of self-management at the grassroots level. The chairman, vice-chairmen and members of each residents' or villagers' committee are elected by the residents. The relationship between residents' and villagers' committees and the grassroots organs of state power is prescribed by law. The residents' and villagers' committees establish sub-committees for public mediation, public security, public health and other matters in order to manage public affairs and social services in their areas, mediate civil disputes, help maintain public order and convey residents' opinions and demands and make suggestions to the people's government.

In 2007, the report of the 17th National Congress of the CPC included, for the first time, the "system of mass self-management at the grassroots level" in the framework of political systems with Chinese characteristics. In 2012, the report of the 18th National Congress of the CPC pointed out that it is imperative to improve the mass organizations of self-management at the grassroots level under the leadership of grassroots organizations of the CPC, and to expand orderly participation, to include more urban and rural residents in managing grassroots-level affairs.

1. Mass self-government at the grassroots level in rural areas

The villagers' committee is the primary mass organization of self-government, in which villagers manage their own affairs, educate themselves and serve their own needs and in which elections are conducted, decisions adopted, administration maintained and supervision exercised by democratic means. The villagers' committee shall manage the public affairs and public welfare undertakings of the village, mediate disputes among villagers, help maintain public order, and convey the villagers' opinions and demands and make suggestions to the people's government.

(1) The composition and function of the villagers' committee

According to the *Organic Law of the Villagers' Committees of the PRC*, a villagers' committee shall be composed of three to seven members, including the chairman, vice-chairman (vice-chairmen) and members. The members of a villagers' committee shall include an appropriate number of women. In a village where people from more than one ethnic group live, they shall include a member or members from the ethnic group or groups with a smaller population. A villagers' committee shall, when necessary, establish sub-committees for public mediation, public security, public health, etc. Members of the villagers' committee may also be members of the sub-committees. The villagers' committee of a village with a small population may dispense with the sub-committees; instead, members of the villagers' committee shall have a division of responsibilities with respect to public mediation, public security, public health, etc.

A villagers' committee and its members shall observe the constitution, the laws, regulations and state policies, comply with and organize the implementation of villagers' autonomy, and village rules and regulations, implement resolutions of the villagers' assembly or the villagers' representatives' assembly, work with integrity, and accept the supervision of the villagers.

(2) Election of a villagers' committee

According to the *Organic Law of the Villagers' Committees of the PRC (2010)*, the chairman, vice-chairman (vice-chairmen) and members of a villagers' committee shall be elected directly by the villagers. No organization or

Chapter 1

individual may designate, appoint or replace any member of a villagers' committee. The term of office for a villagers' committee is three years; a new committee shall be elected at the expiration of the three years without delay. Members of a villagers' committee may continue to hold office when re-elected. Election of a villagers' committee shall be presided over by a villagers' electoral committee. Members of the electoral committee shall be elected by a villagers' assembly or by all the villagers' groups. For election of a villagers' committee, the villagers who have the right to elect in the village shall nominate candidates directly. The number of candidates shall be greater than the number of persons to be elected. Any villager who has reached the age of 18 shall have the right to elect and stand for election, regardless of his ethnic status, race, sex, occupation, family background, religious belief, education, property status and length of residence, with the exception of persons who have been deprived of political rights in accordance with the law. For the election of a villagers' committee, the villagers who have the right to elect in the village shall nominate candidates directly. The villagers' election committee shall organize candidates to meet the villagers, and the candidates shall introduce their ideas of performing their duties and answer questions raised by the villagers.

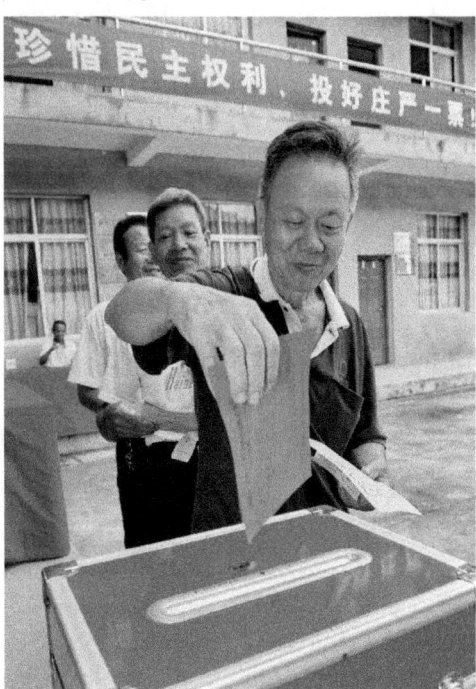

(3) Villagers' representatives assembly

The *Organic Law of the Villagers' Committees of the PRC (2010)* provides that, in a village with a larger population or with inhabitants in a scattered location, villagers' representatives may be elected, and the villagers' committee shall convene a meeting of villagers' representatives to decide on matters through discussion with the authorization of the villagers' assembly. A villagers' representatives meeting is composed of villagers' committee members and representatives of villagers, the villagers' representatives should account for more than four-fifths of the members of the meeting, and more than one-third of the villagers' representatives should be female.

The villagers' representatives meeting shall be convened by the villagers' committee. The meeting should be held once a quarter and should be convened if required by more than one-fifth of villagers' representatives. The villagers' representatives meeting shall set its quorum at two-thirds of all representatives, and all decisions shall pass with a simple majority among representatives present. The villagers' assembly may draft and review the villagers' self-government charters and regulations, and report to the county- or township-level people's government for filing. Charters, pacts, and decisions made by the villagers' assembly or villagers' representatives meeting shall not contravene the constitution, laws, regulations and policies of the state, or infringe upon the villagers' personal rights, democratic rights and legitimate property rights.

2. Mass self-government at the grassroots level in urban areas

An urban residents' committee shall be a mass organization for self-government at the grassroots level in urban areas, in which the residents manage their own affairs, educate themselves and serve their own needs. The people's government of (1) a city that is not divided into districts or (2) a municipal district or (3) an agency of such a people's government shall provide guidance, support and help to the residents' committees in their work. The residents' committees shall, on their part, assist these people's governments or agencies in their work.

(1) The composition and duties of a residents' committee

According to the *Organic Law of the Urban Residents' Committee of the PRC (1989)*, a residents' committee shall be composed of between five and nine members, including the chairman, vice-chairman (vice-chairmen) and members. In areas where people from more than one ethnic group live, the residents' committee shall include a member or members from the group or groups with a smaller population. The chairman, vice-chairman (vice-chairmen) and members of a residents' committee shall be elected by all the residents of a residential area who have the right to elect or by the representatives from all the households; if the residents so require, they may also be elected by the two-to-three elected representatives of residents' groups. The term of office of the residents' committee shall be three years, and its members may continue to hold office when re-elected.

The main duties of residents' committees include: (1) publicizing the constitution, laws, regulations and policies of the state, safeguarding the lawful rights and interests of residents, educating residents for the fulfillment of their statutory obligations and for protecting public property, and conducting various forms of activities for the development of an advanced socialist culture and ideology; (2) handling the public affairs and public welfare services of residents in the local residential area; (3) mediating disputes among residents; (4) assisting in the maintenance of public security; (5) assisting the local people's government or its agency in their work related to the interests of residents, such as public health, family planning, special care for disabled veterans and for family members of revolutionary martyrs and servicemen, social relief, and juvenile education; and (6) conveying residents' opinions and demands and making suggestions to the local people's government or its agency.

Any resident of a residential area who has reached the age of 18 shall have the right to elect and stand for election, regardless of his ethnic status, race, sex, occupation, family background, religious belief, education level, property status and length of residence, with the exception of persons who have been deprived of political rights in accordance with the law.

(2) The residents' assembly

The residents' assembly shall be composed of residents at least 18 years old. It may be attended by all residents at or above the age of 18 or by a representative or representatives of each household; it may also be attended by the elected representatives of residents' groups, numbering two-to-three from each. The quorum for a residents' assembly shall be more than half of the total number of residents at or above the age of 18, or of the representatives of households, or of the representatives elected by residents' groups. Decisions of the residents' assembly shall be adopted by a simple majority of all those present. The residents' committee shall be responsible to the residents' assembly and report on its work to the latter. The residents' assembly shall be convened and presided over by the residents' committee. It shall be convened when proposed by more than one-fifth of residents at or over the age of 18, by more than one-fifth of the number of households, or by more than one-third of the number of residents' groups. When important matters involving the interests of all residents arise, the residents' committee must refer them to the residents' assembly for decision through discussion.

Examples:

Best practices of mass self- government at the grassroots level

1. Jinhua: community meeting on local affairs

On December 31, 2015, the first community meeting on local affairs was held in Dongxiao community, Jindong district, Jinhua city, Zhejiang province. Thirty-one deputies from local urban and rural residents made 17 recommendations and suggestions to the officials present.

The meeting had two items on its agenda: to listen to and discuss the sub-district community office's report on plans regarding economic-social development, budget and key projects and on their implementation; to listen to people's recommendations and suggestions in order to improve the office's work.

2. Xuzhou: bi-monthly work report

In November 2015, the Party Committee of Xuzhou city, Jiangsu province decided that party secretaries, directors, accountants and officials responsible for public order and dispute settlement of urban and rural communities should report their work, in particular on efficiency and integrity, on a bi-monthly basis.

3. Shenzhen, Beijing and Xiamen: separating deliberative and executive organs of the residents' committee

Since 2005, residents committees in Shenzhen, Beijing and Xiamen started a pioneering project to separate the deliberative and executive organs. Community affairs centers were established to complement residents' committees. Ever since then, the committees have been turned into forums to represent the opinions and interests of local residents, who can discuss local affairs in these committees, democratically expressing their ideas and making decisions, while the center is responsible for the implementation of such decisions. Administrative work assigned by local governments is no longer carried out by residents' committees, but by community affairs centers.

4. Dengzhou: the 'four deliberations and two opens' approach

All local affairs in rural communities, under the leadership of a local party committee, must go through four stages of deliberations: local party committee, joint session of the party committee and residents' committee, meeting of party members, and representation of local households or meeting of residents. Decisions must be open, and the implementation and its result must also be open. This approach has stipulated procedures that local authorities must follow, so that major local affairs, in particular those that concern people's interests, can be discussed and decided transparently by the local people themselves.

Chapter 2

China's Governments

This chapter analyses the structure and operational process of the Chinese government. It introduces the features, functions and powers of the central people's government, and analyzes the composition, powers, main functions and operating process of local governments at all levels. It also discusses China's administrative divisions, analyzes the importance of China's 'one country, two systems' policy, and introduces the SARs and the powers they hold.

I. Composition and Powers of the State Council

1. The status of the central government

The State Council, that is, the central people's government, is the executive body of the highest organ of state power; it is the highest organ of state administration.

(1) The State Council is the executive body of the highest organ of state power

Article 85 of the constitution provides that: "The State Council, that is, the central people's government of the PRC is the executive body of the highest organ of state power;[1] it is the highest organ of state administration." The State Council enforces the laws enacted and resolutions adopted by the NPC and its Standing Committee. After the review and approval of the national economic and social development plan and the national budget of the NPC, if changes are involved, they shall be reviewed and approved by the Standing Committee of the NPC and implemented by the State Council. Administrative measures, regulations, decisions and orders of the State Council must be based on the constitution and fundamental laws stipulated by the NPC and other laws enacted by the Standing Committee of the NPC.

---

[1] The constitution provides that the highest organ of state power is the National People's Congress

As the executive body of the highest organ of state power, the State Council is accountable to, and reports to, the NPC. The constitution provides that the NPC decides the choices of officials to the State Council. When the congress is not in session, its Standing Committee shall decide the choice of ministers, directors of commissions, auditor general and secretary general. The congress holds the power to remove State Council officials from office, to supervise the work of the council, and to annul those administrative rules and regulations, decisions or orders of the State Council that contravene the constitution or laws. When the NPC or its Standing Committee is in session, they are entitled to put forward an inquiry against the State Council.

(2) The State Council is the highest organ of state administration

The constitution provides that the State Council shall exercise unified leadership over the work of local organs of state administration at various levels throughout the country, and to formulate the detailed division of functions and powers between the central government and the organs of state administration of provinces, autonomous regions and municipalities directly under the central government, and other policies and measures that have a nationwide influence. As the highest organ of state administration, the State Council has the power to alter or annul inappropriate decisions and orders issued by local organs of state administration at various levels. While being responsible to and reporting to the local organ of state power at the same level, local organs of state administration at all levels shall also be responsible to and report to the organs of state administration at next highest level, as well as following the unified leadership of the State Council.

(3) The State Council enjoys the highest status in the state administration system

The status of the State Council is determined by the constitution, which embodies the characteristics of the unitary system of centralized government. The central government has the absolute and centralized authority and power, and it leads directly or indirectly all the local governments in any place and at any level. The highest administrative status of the State Council means that the administrative authority of the State Council is the highest in the country. The administrative actions taken by the State Council shall have the highest legal and political validity. The central government can take some measures to change the administrative actions of local governments. Within the state administration system, any local government must obey the leadership of the State Council.

2. The composition and term of office of the state council

The State Council is composed of the following: the premier; vice-premiers; state councilors; ministers in charge of ministries; ministers in charge of commissions; the auditor general; and secretary general. The term of office of the State Council is the same as that of the NPC, i.e. five years. After the1982 constitution, the premier, vice-premiers and state councilors shall serve no more than two consecutive terms.

Examples:

Models of auditing

1. Auditing agency as an organ of the legislature

Independent from government, the supreme auditing agency is subordinate to the legislature (parliament), and reports to and is responsible to the legislature. Its main function is to assist the legislature in supervising the government, and influence the decision-making of the legislature to a certain extent. The supreme auditing agency works in accordance with the law, and is free from government intervention. Examples: the US, the UK

2. Auditing agency as an organ of the judiciary branch

The supreme auditing agency is called the Auditing Court, and belongs to the judicial branch or carries out judicial responsibilities. The court holds jurisdiction directly against any matter or person that abuses financial and economic laws and regulation, and it has the power to make a decree absolute. It can audit government institutions and state-owned companies. This model has strengthened the authority and independence of the auditing agency. Example: France

3. Auditing agency as an organ outside the three separated powers

The national auditing agency is independent from legislative, judicial and executive powers. It doesn't listen to the parliament, and nor is it a department of the government. The agency holds an objective and fair stand, and is only responsible to the law. It is not subject to influence from political parties. Examples: Germany, Japan, the Netherlands

4. Auditing agency as an organ of the executive branch

The auditing agency is a part of government, or is under the leadership of one government department. It audits budgetary and financial activities of government departments in accordance with the authorization stemming from national laws. The auditing agency is accountable to the government, and its main objective is to ensure the orderly execution of the government's financial policies, laws, plans and budgets. Example: China, whose National Audit Office operates under the leadership of the premier

3. Powers of the State Council

The State Council holds a broad, comprehensive and unified leadership of state administrative activities, and the indirect powers in order to ensure the enforcement of such a leadership.

(1) Direct powers

Rights to administrative legislation and issue orders The State Council may adopt administrative measures, enact administrative rules and regulations, and issue decisions and orders in accordance with the constitution and the law.

Administrative leadership of the State Council over its institutions and local governments The State Council has absolute leadership over all its institutions and local governments. The premier assumes overall responsibility for the work of the State Council. It exercises unified leadership over the work of national and local organs of state administration. It has the power to regulate the division of functions and powers between the central government and local governments at provincial level (including that of provinces, autonomous regions and municipalities directly under the jurisdiction of the State Council), without consultation with the latter.

Administrative powers The State Council is the highest administrative authority in China. It regulates all administrative affairs of the state, which include: (1) economic affairs and urban and rural development; (2) the affairs of education, science, culture, public health, physical culture and family planning; (3) civil affairs, public security, judicial administration, supervision and other related matters; (4) the building of national defense; (5) affairs concerning the nationalities and to safeguard the equal rights of minority nationalities and the right to autonomy of national autonomous areas; (6) approving the geographic division of provinces, autonomous regions and municipalities directly under the central government, and the establishment and geographic division of autonomous prefectures, counties, autonomous counties and cities; (7) examining and deciding on the size of administrative organs and, in accordance with the law, to appoint or remove administrative officials, train them, appraise their performance and reward or punish them;

and drawing up and implementing the plan for national economic and social development and the state budget.

Foreign affairs The State Council conducts foreign affairs and concludes treaties and agreements with foreign states, and protects the legitimate rights and interests of Chinese nationals living abroad and protects the lawful rights and interests of returned overseas Chinese and of family members of Chinese nationals living abroad.

(2) Indirect powers

Legislative proposals When the State Council is faced with matters that are beyond its scope of authority, it may submit proposals to the NPC or its Standing Committee for legislation or authorization of the NPC or its Standing Committee.

Veto power The State Council may alter or annul inappropriate orders, directives and regulations issued by ministries or commissions; and inappropriate decisions and orders issued by local organs of state administration at various levels.

Emergency mobilization The State Council may determine to exercise emergency mobilization in some parts of provinces, autonomous regions and municipalities directly under the central government. When average administrative means fail, the State Council has the authority to order an emergency mobilization to implement its managerial goals. Emergency mobilization is only applicable in extreme conditions, and is only designed to be a remedy of day-to-day administrative measures.

4. Institutions of the State Council

The State Council is composed of the following institutions: the Ministry of Foreign Affairs, National Development and Reform Commission, Ministry of Defense, Ministry of Education, Ministry of Science and Technology, Ministry of Industry and Information Technology, State Ethnic Affairs Commission, Ministry of Public Security, Ministry of Supervision, Ministry of Civil Affairs, Ministry of Finance, Ministry of Human Resources and Social Security, Ministry of Land and Resources, Ministry of Environmental Protection, Ministry of Housing and Urban-Rural Development, Ministry of Transport, Ministry of Water Resources, Ministry of Agriculture, Ministry of Commerce, Ministry of Culture, National Health and Family Planning Commission, People's Bank of China and National Audit Office.

Chapter 2

Major institutional reforms of the State Council since reform and opening up (1978)

1. The 1982 reform was aimed at tackling bureaucratic empire building and low efficiency. The reform reduced the number of State Council departments from 100 to 61, with a reduction of about 25% of central government positions and a 67% decrease in management posts. Life-long tenure for senior government officials was abolished.

2. The 1988 reform was the first to follow the principle of 'adjusting government functions', and started to establish a national civil service system. The reform reduced the number of State Council departments from 72 to 68.

3. The 1993 reform was focused on transforming government functions by separating government- and state-owned enterprises following the needs of the socialist market economy. The reform reduced the number of State Council departments from 86 to 59, and 80% of central government positions.

4. The 1998 reform was a big step forward in transforming government functions. Nearly all departments dedicated to a certain industry sector were abolished. The reform reduced the number of offices in the State Council to 52, with a 47.5% fall in the number of people employed by the central government. State Council department numbers were reduced from 40 to 29 (General Office excluded).

5. The 2003 reform was put forward after China's accession to the World Trade Organization (WTO). It was aimed at further transforming government functions, improving management approaches, applying e-governance, improving administrative efficiency and reducing costs.

6. The 2008 reform covered 15 departments, with ministerial-level ones abolished. The reform had three main targets: enhancing macro-control to promote scientific development; improving people's livelihoods by strengthening social management and public service; integrating offices of similar functions in an attempt to create departments that cover a larger area and establishing comprehensive offices. The number of State Council departments was reduced to 28.

7. The 2013 reform played a role in further improving the establishment of comprehensive departments focusing on transforming and streamlining

government functions. After the reform, the Ministry of Railways was abolished. The functions of railway planning and policy development were shifted into the Ministry of Transport. A national railway company was created. The National Health and Family Planning Commission, China Food and Drug Administration, and State Administration of Press, Publication, Radio, Film and Television were established. The State Oceanic Administration was reintroduced with the National Oceanic Committee formed as a high-level deliberation and coordination institution. The National Energy Administration, having absorbed the function of the State Electricity Regulatory Commission, which was abolished, was placed under the framework of the National Development and Reform Commission. State Council department numbers were reduced to 25 (General Office excluded).

II. China's Administrative Divisions, Local State Organs and their Functions

1. Administrative divisions in China

Municipalities directly under the central government and other large cities are divided into districts and counties. Autonomous prefectures are divided into counties, autonomous counties and cities. All autonomous regions, autonomous prefectures and autonomous counties are national autonomous areas. The state may establish special administrative regions when necessary. The systems to be instituted in special administrative regions shall be prescribed by law enacted by the NPC in the light of specific conditions.

At present, there are 34 provincial-level administrative regions in China, comprising 23 provinces, five autonomous regions, four municipalities and two special administrative regions. Provincial administrative regions have their traditional and customary acronyms. They have their own capitals where the provincial-level people's governments are located. Beijing, where the central people's government is located, is the capital of China.

The township is China's most basic administrative unit. All autonomous regions, autonomous prefectures and autonomous counties are national autonomous areas. They are all indispensible parts of the motherland. The state may establish SARs when necessary. In addition, the state may make adjustments and changes to the administrative divisions when necessary to improve administration of the economy and ethnical unity.

Chapter 2

Hong Kong and Macau are parts of China's territory. The Chinese government resumed the exercise of sovereignty over Hong Kong after July 1, 1997, when a special administrative region of Hong Kong was established. On December 20, 1999, the Chinese government resumed the exercise of sovereignty over Macau with the establishment of Macau SAR.

2. Local state organs

(1) Provincial-level people's government

China has 23 provincial people's governments, five governments of national autonomous regions, and four governments of municipalities directly under the jurisdiction of the State Council. They are all provincial-level people's governments. The major consideration to establish a province is for territory and society management. Race and the economy, military and supervisory factors are not the main reason. A province-level region usually includes both rural and urban areas. China has 23 provinces: Hebei, Shanxi, Liaoning, Jilin, Heilongjiang, Jiangsu, Zhejiang, Anhui, Fujian, Jiangxi, Shandong, Henan, Hubei, Hunan, Guangdong, Taiwan, Hainan, Sichuan, Guizhou, Yunnan, Shaanxi, Gansu, and Qinghai.

The 1982 constitution and *The Organic Law of the Local People's Congress and Local People's Governments* made new provisions for the composition of provincial people's governments. A provincial-level people's government is composed of the provincial governor, vice-governor, secretary general and the heads of functional departments. The governor and vice-governor of the province are elected by the provincial people's congress, and the candidates are nominated by the presidium of the congress or through a joint nomination of deputies. When the provincial people's congress is not in session and the governor is unable to perform his duties, the Standing Committee of the provincial people's congress shall decide the choice of an acting governor until the next session of the congress, when a by-election will take place. The term of office of the provincial people's government is five years, the same as that of the provincial people's congress.

Autonomous regions According to the constitution and the law on regional national autonomy, an ethnic autonomous region generally features four main factors. First is the establishment of national autonomous areas. Ethnic autonomous areas are the administrative regions where one or more minority nationalities live in the region and exercise regional autonomy in accordance with the law. The establishment of ethnic autonomous areas at a certain administrative level is the basic condition for the enforcement of the system of regional autonomy, which itself constitutes the basic content of the system. Second, the establishment of organs of self-government. In national autonomous areas, these organs are people's congresses and people's governments of autonomous regions, autonomous prefectures and autonomous counties. The people's courts and the people's procuratorates in national autonomous areas are the judicial organs and procuratorial organs of the national autonomous areas that exercise state judicial and procuratorial powers separately, but are not autonomous organs and don't enjoy autonomous rights. Third, the rights to national autonomy. The law on regional national autonomy provides 27 articles regarding autonomous rights of self-government organs in ethnical autonomous regions, covering economic, financial, cultural and educational affairs. Fourth, policy and institutional support of the state. While ensuring the realization of the autonomous rights of self-government organs in China, the central government has a cluster of supporting policies and mechanisms in place, including: a fiscal subsidy policy to make ends meet in regional ethnic autonomy areas and areas where ethnic minority people live in large numbers; special funds and targeted subsidies for ethnic minority areas; national policies to facilitate economic and cultural advancement in these areas; policies to help autonomous regions cultivate ethnic minority officials, experts and skilled workers in considerable numbers; special consideration is given to the current situation in these areas, which results in a halt in the implementation of certain basic state policies.

Examples:

China now has 155 ethnically autonomous regions, including five province-level regions, 30 city-level regions and 120 county-level regions.

Among China's 55 ethnical minority groups, 44 have their own ethnically autonomous region, covering 71% of the total minority population and 64% of China's territorial area.

In places where ethnic minorities live in compact communities but where the establishment of autonomous areas is not feasible because the populations of the ethnic minorities and the areas in which they live are relatively small, or because the populations are scattered, the constitution provides that ethnic townships be established, so that the minority peoples there can also exercise the right to administer the internal affairs of the ethnic group and be the masters of their own areas.

Chapter 2

Municipalities directly under the jurisdiction of the central government These municipalities are put directly under the jurisdiction of the State Council, and are provincial-level administrative regions. Currently, China has four such cities: Beijing, Tianjin, Shanghai and Chongqing. Whereas provinces generally inherit their historic and cultural borders, municipalities are arranged with particular consideration to facilitate the administration or strategy of the central government in some areas of political or geographical importance. Municipalities directly under the jurisdiction of the central government are mostly composed of urban areas, while a province usually contains both urban and rural areas.

Special administrative regions Since ancient times, Hong Kong and Macau have always been parts of the territory of China. The Chinese government resumed the exercise of sovereignty over Hong Kong on July 1, 1997, and that of Macau on December 20, 1999.

Taking into account the history and reality of the situation in Hong Kong and Macau, in order to safeguard national unity and territorial integrity, China decided, in accordance with the provisions of Article 31 of the constitution, to establish SARs in Hong Kong and Macau. In April 1990, the third session of the seventh NPC adopted *The Basic Law Of The Hong Kong Special Administrative Region Of the PRC*, and in March 1993, the first session of the eighth NPC enacted *The Basic Law of Macau Special Administrative Region of the PRC*. Therefore, the state established Hong Kong and Macau SARs on the exact day of the resumption of sovereignty to put into practice the policies of 'one country, two systems', 'letting Hong Kong people administer Hong Kong', 'letting Macau people administer Macau' and 'a high degree of autonomy'.

The policy of 'one country, two systems' means that, under the unified sovereignty of the PRC, highly autonomous SARs will be established in areas such as Hong Kong and Macau to let them have their own capitalist economic and political systems, while the rest of China uses the socialist system. In China, state power belongs to the people, and is delegated to the central (highest) organ of state power and local organs of state power at all levels. Therefore, though with special powers and high autonomy, the SARs remain local administrations, and their relationship with the central government is that between local and central in a unitary system. SARs are not states in a federal system. They are set up according to the provisions of the constitution and their basic laws. Their powers come from the authorization of the central government. SARs are inalienable parts of the PRC under the full sovereignty of the state and subject to the jurisdiction of the central government. The central government is responsible for foreign affairs and defense of the SARs. It appoints chief executives and the principal officials of the SARs, and holds the power to declare a state of emergency in the SARs. It also explains and amends the basic laws.

As provided by the basic laws, the high degree of autonomy enjoyed by the SARs include, first of all, executive power. The Basic Law provides that: "Hong Kong SAR shall be vested with executive power. It shall, on its own, conduct the administrative affairs of the region in accordance with the relevant provisions of this law." The second element is legislative power. "Hong Kong SAR shall be vested with legislative power." With the exception of those that are reserved by the central government and laws that govern the relationship between the central government and the SARs, Hong Kong and Macau can enact laws on other subjects. The third element is independent judicial power, including that of final adjudication. "Hong Kong SAR shall be vested with independent judicial power, including that of final adjudication. The courts of Hong Kong SAR shall exercise judicial power independently, free from any interference. The power of final adjudication of Hong Kong SAR shall be vested in the Court of Final Appeal of the region, which hands out conclusive judgment. Fourth, powers to handle external affairs. It is necessary to allow a certain degree of autonomy in external affairs for Hong Kong SAR to maintain itself as an international trade, financial, aviation and shipping centre, and for Macau SAR to develop in a healthy manner. In general, the central people's government authorizes Hong Kong SAR to: (1) participate in foreign negotiations, international conferences and international organizations; (2) sign international agreements; (3) establish official and semi-official missions of foreign countries; and (4) issue passports and travel documents. Fifth, the high degree of autonomy is reflected in: (1) the executive authorities and legislature of the SAR shall be composed of permanent residents of the SAR; (2) the socialist system and policies shall not be practiced in the SARs, and the previous capitalist system and way of life shall remain unchanged for 50 years; (3) land and natural resources within the SAR shall be state property. The government of the SAR shall be responsible for the management, use and development of its land and for its lease or grant to individuals, legal persons or organizations for use or development. The resultant revenues shall be exclusively at the disposal of the government of the region; (4) the SAR shall have independent finances.

It shall use its financial revenues exclusively for its own purposes, and they shall not be handed over to the central people's government. The central people's government shall not levy taxes in the SAR; (5) the SARs shall have independent monetary systems. The authority to issue Hong Kong dollars and Macau patacas shall be vested respectively in the governments of Hong Kong and Macau SARs; (6) the SARs shall have the right to use, respectively, English in Hong Kong SAR and Portuguese in Macau SAR as an official language. In addition, apart from displaying the national flag and national emblem of the PRC, the SARs may also use a regional flag and regional emblem. It also reflects the high degree of autonomy exercised in SARs.

(2) Municipality-level people's government

A municipality-level people's government is under the jurisdiction of a province or autonomous region. It governs county-level administrative units, including districts, counties and county-level cities. As China gradually shifts to the administrative hierarchy of province-municipality-county-township, municipality-level people's governments are becoming more important as they connect county-level governments and provincial-level ones. A municipality-level people's government is composed of a mayor, vice-mayors, a secretary general, and directors of bureaus and commissions. The mayor and vice-mayors are elected by the people's congress at the same level.

(3) County-level people's government

People's governments of counties, city districts and county-level cities are referred to as county-level people's governments. The county was the earliest administrative division in China's history. Generally, county boundaries will not be altered. After the foundation of the PRC, a dual-track system was adopted, dividing the country into urban and rural areas. As a consequence, counties became more essential in both politics and administration. Counties are responsible for managing rural people and, therefore, they handle a large territory. They became a major contributor to the country's industrialization. After 1983, most counties were put under the direct jurisdiction of municipality-level people's governments.

A county-level city is a small region that meets state requirements for independent jurisdiction. County-level cities are basically composed of urban areas, where the urban economy and culture are well developed. In recent years, some counties have been re-classified as county-level cities based on the county's region of jurisdiction. These county-level cities feature both urban and rural life.

A county-level people's government is the executive organ of a county-level people's congress. Members of the government include county chief and deputy chiefs elected by the People's Congress and heads of offices, commissions and bureaus, who are nominated by the county chief and appointed by the Standing Committee of the People's Congress. A county-level people's government serves a term of five years.

(4) Township-level people's governments

The people's governments of townships, ethnic townships and towns are known as township-level people's governments. A township people's government, which is composed of a township head and several deputy heads elected by the respective people's congress, is the grassroots-level state organ of administration in rural areas. Townships in minority areas are established as ethnic townships. Townships are referred to as towns in urban areas. The difference between a town and a township is that the former governs a certain region in a county that has highly developed industries and business, a highly-concentrated population and relatively developed public facilities.

3. Main functions of local governments

In accordance with the provisions of Article 59 of the *Organic Law of the Local People's Congresses and Local People's Governments of the PRC*, a local people's government at or above county level shall exercise the following functions and powers: (1) to implement the resolutions of the people's congress and its standing committee at the corresponding level as well as decisions and orders of state administrative organs at higher levels; (2) to direct the work of its subordinate departments and of the people's governments at lower levels; (3) to alter or annul inappropriate orders and directives of its subordinate departments and inappropriate decisions and orders of the people's governments at lower levels; (4) to appoint or remove personnel in state administrative organs, train them, appraise their performance and award or punish them according to the provisions of law; (5) to implement a plan for national economic and social development and the budget, and conduct administrative work concerning the economy, education, science, culture, public health, physical culture, protection of the environment and natural resources, urban and rural development, finance, civil affairs, public security, nationality affairs, judicial administration, supervision and family planning within its administrative area; (6) to protect socialist property owned by all the people, property owned collectively by working people and citizens' legitimate private property, and to maintain public order and safeguard citizens' rights and their democratic and other rights; (7) to protect the legitimate rights and interests of various economic organizations; (8) to safeguard the rights of minority nationalities and respect their customs, assist those areas where minority nationalities live in concentrated communities within its sphere of jurisdiction to exercise regional autonomy in accordance with the constitution and other laws and assist the various minority nationalities in their political, economic and cultural development; (9) to safeguard women's rights as endowed by the constitution and other laws, such as equality with men, equal pay for equal work and freedom of marriage; and (10) to handle other matters assigned by state administrative organs at higher levels.

According to Article 61 of the *Organic Law of the Local People's Congresses and Local People's Governments of the PRC*, the people's government of a township, nationality township or town shall exercise the following functions and powers: (1) to implement the resolutions of the people's congress at the corresponding level and the decisions and orders of state administrative organs at higher levels and to issue decisions and orders; (2) to implement the plan for economic and social development and the budget of its administrative area and conduct administrative work concerning the economy, education, science, culture, public health, physical culture, finance, civil affairs, public security, judicial administration and family planning in its administrative area; (3) to protect socialist property owned by all the people, property owned collectively by working people and citizens' legitimate private property and to maintain public order and safeguard citizens' rights of the person and their democratic and other rights; (4) to protect the legitimate rights and interests of various economic organizations; (5) to safeguard the rights of minority nationalities and respect their customs; (6) to safeguard women's rights as endowed by the constitution and the law, such as equality with men, equal pay for equal work and freedom of marriage; and (7) to handle other matters assigned by the people's governments at higher levels.

Chapter 3

China's Public Services System Reform

Public service refers to the actions taken by the public sector, such as government or non-profit organizations, as well as some private organizations, in order to meet the needs of the community and safeguard public interest, and to produce and provide the supply of public goods in accordance with the law. According to the national plan on the basic public services system (2011-2015), public services refer to those that secure the basic survival and development of all citizens are in line with social and economic development, are guided by the government and are based on a certain level of social consensus. It is a citizen's basic right to enjoy basic public services and the government's obligation. Generally, education, social security, health care, family planning, housing, culture and sports, all of which are required for living at a basic level, are regarded as public services. In broader terms, communications, transport, infrastructure and environmental protection are also included due to the fact that they are closely related to people's day-to-day lives. Those services that are needed to ensure security, including police forces, consumer protection and national defense, are also considered public services.

I. Implications of China's Household Registration System on Public Services

The household registration system (*hukou*) is a basic system of state administration. The traditional household registration system is directly related to land, and family is the basic unit in population management. In a modern household registration system, the state collects, confirms and registers basic information on citizens regarding births, deaths, relatives, address, etc, in order to protect the rights and interests of citizens in employment, education, social welfare and so on. This is an approach of population management that is based on individuals.

Chapter 3

1. Historical evolution of China's household registration system

In China, the household registration system was first established in cities and then in rural areas. It can be divided into three stages: in the first stage, focus was given to information registration, and the major purpose of the household registration policy was to record where people live and their basic information – registration was not linked to services, and it didn't impose any restriction on free migration; in the second stage, focus shifted to restricting people from migrating freely, in particular, halting population flow from rural areas to cities; in the third stage, social welfare services, such as employment, education, housing, medical care and social security, were linked to household registration.

On August 12, 1950, the State Public Security Authority issued an internal regulation: *Interim Measures on the Management of People that Need Special Attention (Draft)*, which marked the official start of the household registration system. The aim of building such a system was to consolidate the newly-born regime, and the main task was to maintain social order and to prevent the anti-revolutionists and other enemies from damaging the new society. On July 16, 1951, the Ministry of Public Security adopted the *Provisional Regulations on the Administration of Urban Household Registration (Hukou)*, which was the earliest law on the system, and it unified practice in Chinese cities on *hukou* registration. After the first national census in 1953, the majority of rural areas adopted a simpler registration system. In March 1956, the first national working conference on *hukou* registration was held, in which the three basic functions of the system were put on record: (1) providing proof on one's identity; (2) helping in census statistics; (3) preventing and discovering criminal activities and anti-revolutionists.

While the *hukou* system improved, restrictions on population flow became stricter. When the People's Republic was first founded, free flow between cities and rural areas was allowed, resulting in 15m rural residents moving to the cities. In 1949, the urban population accounted for 10.6% of the total population while, in 1952, that figure increased to 12.5%. China's first five-year plan was implemented in 1953, which saw the first peak of population flow due to a national industrialization strategy that emphasized heavy industry. From 1954 to 1956, each year more than 77m people migrated, and the figure increased for the next three years. Self-motivated migration and organized mass migration planned by the state occurred at the same time.

As China embarked on its heavy industry strategy, cities faced a shortage of food, which forced the state to exercise a monopoly on the food market, thereby widening the price gap between agricultural and industrial products. Seeking a better life, a large number of the excess labor force in rural areas flooded into the cities to find work in industry, causing the urban population to grow and resources to tighten. The state was pressured to take new policies, such as *hukou* control, planned supply of food and edible oil, labor control and social security control, to maintain a healthy level of population influx. The aims of such measures were to reduce the pressures faced by cities and support the state's industrialization strategy.

The State Council promulgated the *Regulations on the Standards for Urban and Rural Areas Demarcation,* according to which, terms such as 'agricultural population' and 'non-agricultural population' were used to facilitate the population census. This marked the establishment of a rural-urban dual-track household registration system, or *hukou*. The Central Committee of the CPC and the State Council issued several orders to prohibit the rural population from fleeing rural areas and industries from hiring rural labor, in order to control population size in cities. Public security authorities were required to tighten *hukou* control, and return the rural population who were living in cities or working in industries to their rural homes. Food authorities in cities were forbidden from supplying food to people who were not registered in those cities.

During the period of national economic adjustment, the state created a set of policies to go alongside *hukou* registration that govern public services, including education, employment, housing and labor protection. *Hukou* was the only criterion for people to benefit from these services. The dual-track system was consolidated. With the *hukou* system as its core, the unique Chinese dual-track system of rural and urban areas was formulated that featured different policies in terms of housing, grain supply, non-grain food and fuel supply, production materials, employment, health care, elderly care insurance, labor protection insurance, marriage and family planning. After the 1975 amendment to the constitution, 'free migration' was outlawed, thus marking the final establishment of such a system that differentiated urban and rural *hukou*.

2. Reform of the household registration (*hukou*) system

The *hukou* system was established under the framework of a planned economy. It has contributed to China's industrialization, yet also caused

Chapter 3

huge damage to society. Thanks to this system, the state was in control of society's resources, to the maximum extent possible. This allowed China to achieve economic takeoff based on a deprived agricultural economy. But at the same time, the system prevented the free flow of the population, which acted as an obstacle to the release of social vitality. As it prevented the rural population from migrating to cities, it protected cities from an excessive population but, at the same time, undermined urbanization and agricultural production. This system was one reason for low agricultural productivity, rural poverty and the large gap between rural and urban areas. After the reform and opening up, China strived to put in place a market economy with socialist characteristics and, with that process, the *hukou* system revealed many problems. The underlined rationale of this system contravened the regular pattern of modernization and the equality that socialism pursues. The *hukou* system is now an institutional obstacle to China's modernization. To reform the system, the fundamental idea is to safeguard citizen's freedom of migration and residence.

At present, China is promoting an unprecedented reform of the *hukou* system that is based on the gradual evolution of the market economy. In order to promote social justice, China will no longer connect *hukou* with social welfare, and therefore reduce the gap between cities and rural areas. Local governments in China have carried out a series of innovations in the reform. There are three main measures.

(1) Residence permit system

By holding a residence permit, the citizen can enjoy the benefits of local residents in areas such as employment and day-to-day life. On February 23, 2009, Shanghai municipal government issued the *Regulation on the Application for Permanent Household Registration (Hukou) in Shanghai by Residence Permit Holders*. It requires that, after seven years holding a residence permit, the holder can apply for permanent registration. If the quota for the current year is full, they may apply in the following year.

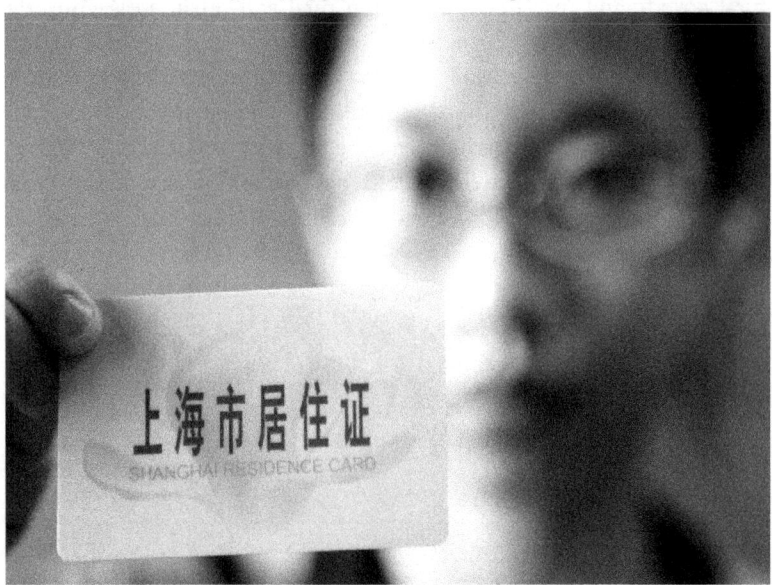

(2) Credit system

A reform mechanism in Guangdong and other areas that non-locally registered people who are working or doing business in the area can apply for permanent registration by collecting credits according to a set of rules.

(3) Unified urban and rural registration

After October 2008, Jiaxing city in Zhejiang province started to implement a uniformed urban and rural household registration system and abolished the distinction of agricultural and non-agricultural registration. The city has since been exercising the same registration and migration policy in both rural and urban areas. If an applicant has a legal and stable residence as well as a stable job (or a stable source of income), he or she will be allowed to register permanently in the city.

After January 1, 2009, Qiqihar city started to push forward *hukou* reform. This led to a unified system of registration in both urban and rural areas, as well as *hukou* transfer. The main content of the reform includes: (1) establishing a unified system of registration in both urban and rural areas; (2) abolishing the distinction between agricultural and non-agricultural registration; (3) abandoning the dual-tracked *hukou* system and referring to all citizens as 'Qiqihar residents'.

3. Cancellation of the dual-tracked *hukou* system

On July 30, 2014, the State Council published *Opinions on the Further Promotion of Hukou Reform* and announced the further reform of the household registration system that marked the full implementation of the reform. *Hukou* reform concerns the wellbeing of hundreds of millions of people and is an important reform at the fundamental level. It is unprecedented in terms of scale, government commitment and coverage. The most essential part of the reform is to build a unified *hukou* registration system in both rural and urban areas. This means that the dual-tracked *hukou* system that differentiates between 'agricultural' and 'non-agricultural' registration will be abolished. Some relevant policies, such as Blueprint Hukou, which was adopted as an interim measure to facilitate migrants, will also be cancelled. From now on, every citizen in China will be registered as 'residents', and *hukou* will be used generally as population statistics. It has been made clear that the statistical system that goes in line with the new system in education, health care, family planning, social security, housing, land and population sectors will be put in place.

II. Measures Taken by the Chinese Government to Promote the Equalization of Basic Public Services

China promotes the equalization of basic public services, aimed at gradually building a uniform basic public services system in both rural and urban areas according to the national plan of major function area development and regional development strategy. It also seeks to encourage the balanced allocation of public service resources between rural and urban areas and among regions to reduce the gap in the quality.

1. Promoting the equalization of public services in urban and rural areas

(1) Strengthening the unified planning of urban and rural basic public services

Public services planning must be conducted in terms of population and space.

Urban and rural areas will be provided with basic public services according to one unified standard set on infrastructure and personnel.

(2) Promoting the convergence of urban and rural basic public service system

Incremental targets will be set to promote the establishment of a unified public system in urban and rural areas. Local governments will be encouraged to create pilot reform projects and include rural residences in urban public services if local conditions so permit. If not, local authorities are required to reduce the service gap between rural and urban areas, and pay attention to future institutional building.

(3) Increasing support to basic public services in rural areas

More resources, especially state funds, will be allocated to rural areas, which will make rural areas an investment priority. State authorities will publish lists of services and their standards to help promote professionalism at the rural grassroots level. Government will encourage and guide high quality public service resources in urban areas to cover rural areas by means such as information technology and mobile services so that rural areas can share the same high quality resources enjoyed in cities.

(4) Accelerating public service coverage for migrant workers and other migrants for an eventual coverage of all residents and underscoring the responsibilities of receiving governments

While reforming and improving the *hukou* and rural land management system, steps will be taken to delink basic public services from household registration and ensure that qualified migrants can enjoy basic public services (BPS) as equally as local residents. Effective measures will be taken to include qualified migrant workers and their children in the BPS system of their residence area in an incremental manner and with special needs highlighted.

2. Promoting the equalization of BPS among regions

(1) Promoting BPS in main function areas

BPS capacity will be enhanced to match the needs arising from industrialization and urbanization with BPS infrastructure, supply, population distribution, environment and transport in priority areas and key areas of development. State funding will be increased with strengthened transfer payment to ensure BPS in areas where development is restricted or prohibited.

(2) Increase BPS support to areas with special needs

State BPS funding and public resources will be channeled to poverty-stricken areas, old revolutionary base areas, ethnic minority areas, border areas and large-scale areas with special needs. These areas will enjoy priority in state BPS investment. Development areas will be encouraged to partner with these areas in various ways to support long-term BPS advancement.

(3) Establishing and improving the coordination mechanisms for the equalization of BPS among regions

Consultation and coordination between the departments of the State Council and provincial governments will be strengthened to keep overall coherence among regions in terms of the scope and standards of BPS. Policies in investment, taxation, industry, land and population will be better coordinated. A BPS management mechanism with local governments as its core will be established to emphasize the role of provincial governments in promoting BPS equalization within the provincial-level areas. In order to support regional integration, measures will be taken to enhance regional coordination in BPS supply, resource sharing and institutional streamlining. Developed areas, such as the Yangtze River and Pearl River deltas, will be encouraged to be the first regions to achieve equal access to BPS.

3. Reforming the public finance system to strengthen support to BPS

An escalating mechanism of BPS expenditure will be set up to promote the capacity of state funding, particularly at county level, to support BPS. The increase should be in line with economic development and the increase of government revenue.

(1) Clarifying the responsibilities and rights to spending between central and local government

Laws will be enacted in a gradual manner to regulate a reasonable match of responsibilities undertaken by central and local governments and their rights to spending, taking into account existing laws, beneficiaries, costs and efficiency, with priority given to the grassroots level. The central government shall be responsible for making fundamental national BPS standards and regulations, providing BPS that should be governed at central level, coordinating BPS issues that go beyond provincial borders, supervising BPS provided by provincial-level governments and holding them accountable. Provincial-level governments shall be responsible for regulating elementary BPS standards and local regulations, providing BPS that should be governed at provincial level, supervising BPS provided by county-level and city-level governments and holding them accountable. County-level and city-level governments are responsible for providing local BPS and supervising BPS agencies.

Responsibilities that are more conducive to be undertaken by provincial or central governments will be transferred from local governments in a gradual way with corresponding rights to spending. Province-level governments will have more spending responsibilities in providing BPS in education, employment, social security and health care.

(2) Improving the transfer payment system and improving the combination of general payments and targeted payments

After clarifying the responsibilities of all levels of governments in BPS and matching relevant rights to spending, the central government will subsidize local governments on BPS that belong to the jurisdiction of local governments through general transfer payments, arrange sufficient funding through targeted transfer payments for missions committed by the central government, and pay according to an agreed ratio the part that should be covered by the central government in terms of BPS that are co-governed by the local and central government.

Methods to accomplish transfer payment will be improved. More payments will be done as general arrangements, in particular those that are aimed to help local governments make ends meet. More funds will be transferred to central and western areas, in particular those areas where development is restricted or prohibited. Targeted transfer payments will be streamlined to improve the equalization of BPS.

The sub-provincial-level transfer payment system will be enhanced at a faster rate. Provincial-level governments will be boosted to make good use of sub-provincial-level transfer payments to reduce the gap in funding of BPS among regions in provincial-level areas. In areas where counties are put under the direct financial jurisdiction of provinces, special emphasis will be given to counties through transfer payment, while in other areas, provincial-level and municipal-level governments shall take all kinds of methods to increase transfer payments to county-level governments.

(3) Improving financial support

Public budgeting will be improved to optimize spending structure. Governments at all levels shall make BPS a priority in budget making, ensure a corresponding increase in BPS spending with revenue and BPS needs, and arrange BPS spending based on the number of local residents. A redistribution adjustment mechanism that is led by the government and underscores social justice will be accelerated.

Provide more funds to BPS State funding from the central government will be channeled to poverty-stricken areas and bottlenecks in the BPS supply chain to enhance BPS supply. All levels of local government, especially provincial-level governments, shall arrange matching funds. BPS investment will be increased thanks to effective financing from a wider range of sources, such as loans from the International Monetary Fund. A larger proportion of state revenue from state-owned enterprise profits will be allocated to enhance BPS. The scale of the national social security fund will be expanded.

Enhance the capacity of county-level government funds to support BPS The central government makes regulations on the scale and standards for publicly-funded BPS at county-level and adjust according to policy changes and other factors. Provincial- and municipal-level governments shall increase fund allocation to subordinate county-level governments, aimed at guaranteeing BPS supply, in particular in poverty-stricken counties. County-level governments shall exercise more stringent discipline, better coordinate finance resources and apply standardized budget management. The central government shall establish an incentive and commitment mechanism to ensure that county-level governments provide enough funding for BPS, and award them accordingly.

4. Searching for new supply modals and supply mechanisms with diverse sources

(1) Allow more private capital in BPS supply after ensuring effective supervision of the government, strict self-regulation of agencies and strong monitoring of the public

State authorities and local governments shall take non-public institutions into consideration in planning and allocating BPS resources, especially in introducing new supply. Private capital will be allowed to host BPS agencies and provide BPS to the public, and encouraged to take part in the building, management and operation of BPS agencies. Private kindergartens and vocational training agencies will be key areas for private capital entry on an equal footing. Private capital will also be encouraged to open hospitals, joint venture with public hospitals, set up care centers for the elderly and disabled, and build museums and gymnasiums.

(2) Actively promote BPS supply by means of government-purchased services, franchising, contracting, outsourcing and land transfer agreements

Policy specifics, including standards and requirements for entry, qualifications, registration, approval, bidding, service supervision, awarding, punishing and quitting shall be developed for different market sectors. Private BPS entities shall enjoy the same status as state-owned agencies in terms of requirements, qualifications, employee's professional development, taxation and application for becoming vendors of government-purchased services.

(3) Give full play to the guiding and regulating role of public investment

Make good use of government subsidy to balance supply and need in the BPS market, develop pilot projects of state fund-subsidized non-public BPS agencies, and actively look into the possibility of direct subsidies to BPS beneficiaries in order to give them more choice and foster a more flexible market in which BPS agencies can compete with each other on an equal footing.

(4) Improve BPS capacity of communities and build a community-based social management and public service platform in urban and rural areas

In building a community service system, residents' needs must be underscored, BPS supply synthesized and BPS infrastructure built according to local conditions. General BPS supply, grassroots-level administration, social security, health care, family planning, cultural activities, sport events and science promotion can share the same building. In rural areas where many residents are migrant workers, emphasis should be placed on taking care of their family members who are still living in the area. After concentrating the above-mentioned services, excess resources should be channeled to elderly care and nursery services. More professional social workers will be trained to guide local volunteers.

(5) Improve IT application in BPS

A national digital training database and public education service platform will be built. IT systems on employment management, social security, BPS, health care, population and family planning, government-subsidized housing, and cultural and sport events will be improved to achieve coherence and information sharing. The application of IT will be leveraged to improve efficiency of public service agencies, and develop new service and business models.

Chapter 4

China's Education Reform

The Ministry of Education (MoE) is in charge of planning, coordinating and managing education in China. It is the State Council's administrative authority in education. Provinces, cities and counties have corresponding education divisions, commissions, bureaus or offices. They are subordinate organs of the MoE. China's education system is split into five stages: pre-primary education (for 3-5-year-olds), primary education (6-11), secondary education (12-17), higher education and continuous education. Mainstream secondary schools are further divided into junior and senior secondary schools, each lasting for three years. Some junior secondary graduates continue their studies in senior high schools, while others do so in professional high schools and secondary-level vocational schools. In China, universities, colleges and higher vocational institutes provide higher education. Continuous education is further divided into skills training for adults, non-degree higher education for adults and literacy education.

I. Evolution of China's Education Strategy

Since the reform and opening up, the Chinese government has kept education a priority and assigned it strategic importance. As early as in the 1990s, the government put forward strategies such as '科技是第一生产力' ('science and technology constitute a primary productive force'), '科教兴国' ('national rejuvenation through science and education'), and 'determined to develop an education that meets modern, world and future standards'.

The former general secretary of the CPC, Jiang Zemin, made it clear that education is essential in improving science, technology and creativity. Education is the main channel to the creation, spread and application of knowledge. It helps to cultivate highly skilled workers and specialists, strengthen creativity and create more technical innovation.

China faces long-standing problems in its economic development, which requires education to solve. China's economy is characterized by large scale but low per capita figures. It faces a scarcity of resources in per capita terms, but per unit resource consumption remains high. It produces many goods, but lacks high-level scientists and independent innovation. It faces a heavy burden in providing employment to its large population, while many low-caliber workers make structural unemployment worse. In resolving this contradiction, the government believes education plays a key role: (1) to cultivate professional talent and create knowledge, and promote scientific and technological progress; (2) to allow people to receive more years of education, postpone employment and thus relieve the employment burden; (3) to enhance training, skills and the re-employability of workers, and help them adapt to technological progress and structural adjustment; (4) to provide new economic growth points and new employment opportunities by cultivating entrepreneurship. Therefore, it is essential to achieve universal elementary education to improve the general skills of the workforce as a whole.

In 2010, the Central Committee of the CPC and the State Council issued *National Long-term Outline Planning on Talent Development (2010-2020)* and *National Outline Planning on Long-term Education Reform and Development (2010-2020)*. The two plans show that, by 2020, China will have 180m skilled professionals who will contribute 35% of economic growth, and 20% of the labor-age population will have received higher education; both these percentages are twice as high as the current figure. *National Outline Planning on Long-term Education Reform and Development (2010-2020)* sets a strategic target for China's education reform: to cultivate strong human resources by creating a learning society and achieving modern education. A new outline is proposed: to prioritize development, put people first, underscore reform and innovation, and promote equality and quality. The theme of the reform is to emphasize a people- and quality-oriented education. It is one of China's national, fundamental policies to promote equal access to compulsory education (CE) for everyone to enjoy high-quality and equal education.

II. Main Achievements of CE in China
1. Full coverage of nine-year CE

In 1949, 80% of China's population were illiterate, and the enrolment rate at primary school was less than 20%, while the equivalent figure for junior secondary school was only 6%. Facing this reality, the CPC and government started to promote education as part of a campaign to cultivate civic virtues. China adopted its first law on CE in 1985, followed by an initiative to popularize nine-year CE. By 2000, China had accomplished the two goals of 'full coverage of nine-year CE, and the elimination of illiteracy in the labor force', which meant that 85% of the Chinese people had received nine-year CE and fewer than 5% of working-age people were illiterate. China is one of the best-performing countries in terms of the coverage and quality of nine-year CE among nine densely populated developing countries. By the end of 2002, that figure was raised to 91%.

2. Providing free CE in urban and rural areas

At its 16th national congress, the CPC decided to gradually implement free CE in both urban and rural areas. In 2003, the State Council convened the first national work conference on education in rural areas. It put education in rural areas as a top priority of national strategy and decided that newly added funds in education would mostly be channeled into rural areas. By the end of 2005, the State Council decided to establish the new mechanism of CE spending in rural areas that required both central and local governments to be responsible according to a pre-set proportion and list of spending items. In the same year, the policy of 'two exemptions and one subsidy', which means free tuition and free books and a subsidy to boarding students, came into

force in 592 national key counties of poverty alleviation. It was expanded to the entire country by spring 2007. From 2006 to 2011, a total of Rmb600bn was allocated through targeted funds for CE in rural areas, which served as a stable source of funding for this policy. On September 1, 2008, 28m CE students in urban areas stopped paying for their tuition, which meant that more than 160m students in rural and urban areas were no longer asked to pay tuition fees. That marked the full implementation of free CE in China. This was an important milestone in China's education development, and will help improve people's wellbeing.

3. Full realization of the two goals

The state took an initiative to achieve the two goals of 'full coverage of nine-year CE, and elimination of illiterate people in the labor force' in western areas, which resulted in an increase in coverage from 77% to 98%. Over recent years, tens of billions or renminbi have been invested to improve teaching conditions, including more than 8,000 boarding schools in rural, ethnic minority and border areas. A total of more than Rmb11bn was spent on a modern distance education project for primary and secondary schools in rural areas to allow children in the countryside to share high quality education resources through a long-distance education network. By the end of 2008, 99.3% of China's population, living in 3,038 counties, and accounting for 99.1% of all counties, achieved the two goals. In November 2011, China accomplished the two goals at a national level, which was a historic success in education.

III. Major Obstacles and Countermeasures in Promoting Equal Access to CE in China

It should be noted that, in promoting equal education, basic national conditions, including economic, social, cultural and historical ones, should be respected. China will long be in the primary stage of socialism, which means it will face long-term resource restraints. Education equality doesn't mean providing the same education to each student but, instead, education opportunities and conditions that fit students' overall development.

The main problems promoting CE in China are: (1) China is a developing country with a large population, the state is short of funds and providing CE to a large population is costly; (2) development remains imbalanced among regions, especially due to the distinctive policy framework in urban and rural areas, resulting in the imbalanced development of education in the two areas;

(3) deciding on how to treat children of migrant workers in cities and those of poverty-stricken families fairly; (4) a system needs to be established to ensure fairness in education.

In view of these major problems, the Chinese government has taken a series of measures to promote equal CE.

1. Increase investment and reform financial support to CE

After the reform and opening up, the rapid development of the national economy led to an increase in national revenue, which made more state investment in CE possible. The state has made CE a spending category in the national budget, and all levels of government are increasing spending in this regard every year. From 2006 to 2011, national financial support to CE increased from Rmb330.5bn to Rmb973.9bn, with an average annual growth rate of 24.1%; special transfer payment funds for CE from the central government increased from Rmb18.77bn to Rmb114.05bn, with an average annual growth rate of 43.5%; per capita public spending for primary and junior secondary students went up from Rmb271 and Rmb378 to Rmb1,366 and Rmb2,045 respectively, with an average annual growth rate of 38.2% and 40.1%.

According to the *National Outline Planning on Long-term Education Reform and Development (2010-2020)*, state investment in education shall not fall below 4% of GDP, which was achieved in 2012.

2. Reduce the gap between urban and rural areas to promote fair CE

The imbalanced development of CE remains the major problem. CE constitutes a part of basic public services provided by the government, and is an essential basic service that is free of charge. Promoting equal access to CE has become a joint initiative of education authorities and other government departments.

(1) Reforming state funding to CE in rural areas

In 2005, the State Council issued the *Announcement on Deepening the Reform of Safeguarding CE Funding in Rural Areas*, which decided to include CE spending in rural areas into the national public budgeting system. Spending is covered jointly by central, provincial, city and county (district) governments according to a negotiated proportion or spending subjects. Currently, CE funds are managed by provincial governments and paid largely by county-level governments.

(2) Providing standardized equipment in schools

This is viewed as a basis to promote balanced development of CE. In 2010, the state launched a project to build standardized schools for CE valued at Rmb8.3bn a year in rural areas, with progress made.

(3) Encouraging two-way flow of urban and rural teachers

To promote the balanced development of CE in urban and rural areas, achieving balanced allocation of teaching forces is the key. On the one hand, seconding mechanisms of CE teacher and school masters are established and improved in all areas, allowing them to teach and work alternately in urban and rural schools with the same pay and welfare. Teachers in urban schools must go to rural areas or schools with difficulties for a certain period if they want to apply for senior titles. Enough teachers should be provided to rural schools or those with difficulties, and more training opportunities will be created for teachers. On the other hand, teachers' colleges enroll students with full scholarship. They are going to join schools in rural areas after their graduation. More college graduates are encouraged to teach in rural areas as volunteers.

(4) Regulating admission

The state regulates that CE students should be admitted without formal exams and according to geographic proximity. Local government should regulate catchments and quotas, taking into account student numbers and school distribution. This is a counter-measure to the problem of 'school selection' in urban areas.

3. Support vulnerable groups to ensure fairness in CE

(1) Ensuring the rights of migrant workers' children

Every year, more migrant workers go to cities as urbanization and excessive labor transfer accelerates. Providing education to their children is another issue. The Chinese government therefore amended the *Law on Compulsory Education of the PRC* that requires local governments and public schools in the places where migrants work to ensure their children's rights to CE, despite the fact that they are not registered at the place under the *hukou* system. A special fund has been set up to provide financial support to urban schools that accept migrant children. More policies are coming out from local governments to help.

Chapter 4

(2) Stressing the responsibility of governments in receiving places

First, local governments should include migrant children in their planning and state funding of CE, and provide subsidies to local schools with large numbers of migrant children. Governments should set charging standards for migrant children receiving CE in local schools, and they shall pay no more than local students. Measures should be taken to help migrant children from poverty-stricken families to receive CE. Second, public schools should take the main responsibility in lowering the threshold and reducing the paperwork needed for migrant children to attend local school. A number of schools will be newly built or revamped to accept more migrant children. Third, encourage and support privately-funded schools. Institutional reforms will take place to include migrant children schools in the framework of government support, providing more guidance and assistance in terms of approval, venue, funding and teacher training. Fourth, to further *hukou* reform. Ease regulation terms to allow easier *hukou* registration in small-to-medium-sized cities and towns, making more excess labor in agriculture eligible to register in urban areas and therefore their children to urban schools. The Chinese government has taken a series of measures to generally ensure that every child is admitted to CE.

(3) Providing state scholarship and encouraging private scholarship to ensure children from poverty-stricken families can pursue education

An important feature of equal education is that no child will be out of school just because he or she is born into a poor family. With the development of the state scholarship system, CE students are no longer required to pay for their tuition. In rural areas, students receive free textbooks, and those boarding students, if they come from poverty-stricken families, also enjoy living allowances. Secondary vocational school students in both rural and urban areas are entitled not only to a tuition waiver, but also living and accommodation allowances. The state provides scholarships of this kind to nearly 12m students every year, covering 90% of secondary vocational school students.

Thanks to economic development, the state now is able to provide more subsidies to students. Living allowances to boarding students coming from rural, poverty-stricken families have been increased. The amount of subsidy is linked to economic growth and that of government revenue according to central and local government regulations. Policy frameworks and arrangements are made in both central and local levels to ensure that these funds are allocated on time. All these have safeguarded that children from rural or poverty-stricken families can afford basic civic and vocational education, and that future workers will have better skills.

In addition, the state also encourages the private sector to invest in education. Social forces have long played an important role in financing students from families with economic difficulties. For example, the Hope Project has raised more than Rmb5.6bn, which has funded more than 15,900 primary schools and helped more than 3.4m children over 20 years. In future, it is essential to continue this policy and put forward more measures to create a good ambience for education.

4. Improve the education policy system to fundamentally guarantee fairness in CE

In the *Decision of the Central Committee of the CPC on Some Major Issues Concerning Comprehensively Deepening Reform* adopted at the third plenary session of the 18th central committee of the CPC in 2013, it states that China "will vigorously promote educational equality, improve the financial assistance system for students from families with financial difficulties, and establish an effective mechanism to expand the coverage of high-quality education resources by means of information technology, so as to gradually narrow the gaps between different regions, between urban and rural areas and between different schools. We will make a balanced allocation of compulsory education resources between urban and rural areas, set unified standards for the construction of public schools, exchange principals and teachers among different public schools, and abolish the practice of establishing key schools or classes, so as to overcome the problem caused by choosing schools and reduce the academic burden on students".

The development of modern educational technology and modern distance education networks will bring about a revolutionary reform of education, leading to a learning society in which every citizen can learn. It will also provide new technical methods and approaches for poverty-stricken and remote areas to share in high-quality education resources. China will build a modern network of long-distance education based on China Education and Research Network and satellite video systems that cover the entire nation to give every member of society access to all sorts of education services, regardless of geographical and time constraints.

Besides, establishing a supervision system and indexing review system to promote cross-checking among the government, society, schools and education receivers will be an important guarantee to promote fair education. China needs to put in place a sound review mechanism for educational fairness. It will first establish identification indicators to assess efforts taken by all levels of governments to promote fair education. A data platform will be created to facilitate education institutions and receivers to review government actions. Accountability will be enhanced by linking review results with the performance assessment of local officials. Second, better indicators will be set up to allow education receivers to review the efforts of education institutions. Current indicators, such as enrolment rates to higher-level schools, performance in state exams, and results in math Olympiads will no longer be underscored. Instead, more weight will be given to a school's respect for regulations, its internal rules, supervision and assessment, teacher performance, creativity in teaching and helping students achieve overall development.

An innovation-driven economy is inseparable from good education and scientific research, which are important factors in economic advancement. That will not be achieved without reforms in economic, R&D and education establishment. These reforms are urgently required due to the pressing need to upgrade China's economy and long-term strategy for the 21st century. The ultimate goal of education is to cultivate people who are fully developed, down to earth and can meet the practical needs of society.

Chapter 5

China's Public Employment Service Reform

Public employment service (PES) refers to the establishment of government organizations in order to promote employment. China's *Regulations on Labor Market Management* defines PES as "services provided by labor security departments at all levels, including employment, career guidance, employment training, community employment development services and others". This chapter will first focus on the basic content and policy framework of China's PES system. Second, it introduces the main approaches to promote public employment service in China from the aspects of employment assistance, public employment training, entrepreneurial services and government-purchased employment services. Finally, it analyses the institutional mechanisms for the promotion of employment and entrepreneurship in China.

I. PES System in China

China has the world's largest population of more than 1.3bn. It also has the largest workforce. Efforts to expand employment and meet the needs of employment are an important long-term task for the Chinese government. At present, the Chinese government adopts a more proactive employment policy that features: (1) encouraging workers to find a job first; (2) requiring workers to take the main responsibility of finding a job; (3) letting the market adjust employment; (4) the government in charge of promoting employment and encouraging entrepreneurship. This requires the government to continually strengthen PES, improve the employment environment, and establish and improve a more efficient and higher quality PES system.

With the deepening of reform and opening up, China's PES organizations gradually formed a network to provide free-of-charge PES for the purpose of promoting employment. The main carrier of China's PES is PES agencies established by the government, and its purpose, nature, tasks and services provided are essentially different from private employment agencies and services. Since the end of the 1970s, China has established integrated services in governments higher than county (district) levels that include PES division in labor security authorities, human resource exchange service set up by human resource authorities, employment services for graduates by education authorities and employment services for people with disabilities organized by their federation. In levels below counties, grassroots employment services are also in place. Organizations that provide employment training and entrepreneurial service are established as a supplement. In China, the PES hierarchy now has five levels of management and six levels of service that cover central, provincial, city, district (county), sub-district (town) and community (village) levels. PES professionals include employment instructors, labor security assistants and employment information analysts. Around 98% of sub-districts, 96% of towns and 95% of communities in China have PES institutions.[2]

At present, PES agencies in China are mainly responsible for employment registration, unemployment registration and management. They provide free career guidance, other advice on government policies, information on employment, job supply and demand, government guides on wages and professional training. Other services include employment assistance, business services, unemployment insurance, government-subsidized training, human resources and social security, personal file management, examination and certification, and expert services.

Since the 1990s, with the formulation of a proactive employment policy and the improvement of the law system with the *Law on Employment Promotion* as its core, a PES system has been established as a pro-public good framework. It provides free services to workers, gives employment aid to people who have difficulty in finding jobs, runs employment management and unemployment registration systems for individuals and companies, offers targeted services to people with special needs, releases information to the general public and carries out overall management of PES.

II. Key Services Provided by the PES System in China
1. Employment assistance

Employment assistance is provided by the Chinese government to people who have difficulty in finding jobs. The government sets up a series of

---

[2] http://news.xinhuanet.com/fortune/2012-11/02/c_113584973.htm (February 17, 2013)

targeted support policies, develops community service jobs and provides the unemployed with tailored aid to help them find jobs as soon as possible. The *Law on Employment Promotion* stipulates that people who have difficulty in finding jobs and zero employment families are key groups for the PES system.

At present, the system is carried out mainly through three channels. First, through tax and fee reductions, loans with discounted interest, social insurance subsidies and other preferential policies, the government encourages people having difficulty in getting jobs to find work by themselves or set up their own businesses. Second, the government provides tax incentives, social security subsidies and guaranteed small loans to companies to encourage them to hire people having difficulty in finding jobs. Third, the government develops community services posts and arranges work for people having difficulty in finding jobs. This is the main channel to provide jobs to this group of people, and a last resort in employment assistance.

PES agencies give four kinds of help: (1) personalized one-on-one employment consulting to understand how employment difficulties have arisen, along with job-seekers' abilities and needs; relieve psychological pressure and help them change their mentality and find suitable resolutions; (2) sustained guidance and service after employment to coordinate newly emerged problems; for those who fail to adapt to their new jobs, again provide guidance and employment recommendations to help them find new jobs; (3) maintains close cooperation with local companies and organizations to

develop jobs that are suitable to people having difficulty in finding jobs; (4) organizes regular employment events. Local PES agencies also help university graduates who are unable to find jobs. A dynamic monitoring system is in place to help families whose members are all out of work in a timely manner.[3]

2. Public employment training

In order to promote the healthy development of the labor market and improve the quality of the labor force, China has gradually established a government-led public employment training system. This system plays a positive role in promoting the employment and entrepreneurship of workers, and enhancing the sustainability of employment.

China's public employment training can be classified into four categories: first, targeted training projects that are commissioned by employment service agencies to training institutions to help the unemployed improve their employability. These projects are mainly arranged to train registered unemployed people, including those in cities and towns, excess labor in rural areas, and newly matured laborers who are not employed to become skilled laborers who hold certificates required for special jobs that are identified by government human resources and social security departments. They are largely carried out by designated institutions, including technical schools, training centers set up by government human resources and social security departments, privately funded vocational schools, vocational senior secondary schools, secondary professional schools, and other lawful institutions. Second, employment apprenticeships that are targeted at the urban unemployed, excess workers in rural areas, new graduates or senior students in higher education, students at secondary vocational and professional school, and graduates of secondary schools who want to find a job instead of pursuing higher education. Companies recruit interns and provide onsite training on technology, theory and operational skills. After assessment, interns will be accepted as employees. Third, entrepreneurship training that is provided to people who are willing to open their own business. The urban unemployed, retired serviceman, migrant workers, higher education and technical school students and other members of special groups, such as ex-convicts and people with disabilities, are eligible. This service is also provided to managers of

---

[3] *The Law on Employment Promotion* provides that any urban resident family in which all family members of legal working age are unemployed shall apply for employment assistance to the public employment service institution on the street or community in which the family resides. Where the public employment service institution concerned is satisfied that the family meets the relevant criteria, it shall provide at least one family member with an appropriate position

small-to-medium-sized enterprises and the self-employed. Fourth, subsidies provided to trainees in designated institutions, including skill training for rural laborers, elementary-to-medium level professional certificate training, vocational training for average senior secondary school graduates, as well as diploma programs such as MPA, MBA and EMBA.

In order to help people with employment difficulties, the Chinese government started a series of public employability training programs in the late 1990s, which include re-employment training programs and skills for employment programs for former state-owned enterprise staff, special training programs for transferred rural workers and employment skill training programs for excess workers in rural areas, and special vocational training as a response to the 2008 financial crisis.[4] All these have helped to enhance trainee skills, and open them to a wider range of employment opportunities that provide more stable jobs and a better income.

3. Entrepreneurial services

The report of the 18th congress of the CPC explicitly asked workers to change their idea of employment, and encouraged more forms of employment and entrepreneurship in order to promote employment. In recent years, the Chinese government at all levels has issued a series of policies and measures to promote the development of small and medium-sized enterprises and various types of business groups to enhance services provided to entrepreneurs. In 2008, the *Guidance on Promoting Entrepreneurship in a Bid to Boost Employment* was issued, releasing a clearer blueprint on supportive policies to entrepreneurs, entrepreneurial training and services. Since 2009, 85 cities in 27 provinces and autonomous regions have taken an initiative to create entrepreneur-friendly cities. Sectoral, regional and operational obstacles were cleared and streamlined, areas and sectors that were not legally prohibited to private investors were opened for new company registration, and policies such

---

[4] In 2009, Chengdu city launched a special vocational training program to encourage urban and rural workers who have lost their jobs due to the impact of the international financial crisis to find work. This was the first emergency response program in the country that gave workers training vouchers to improve their employment potential

as guaranteed small loans, fiscal subsidies on interest, and government sites were put into practice. Preferential measures and fee reductions were granted to entrepreneurs in business and commercial management, taxation and bank lending. Government services were improved, including joint approval, one-stop service and making service commitments to facilitate entrepreneurs.

At present, China's entrepreneurial services are mainly provided in three ways.

(1) Preferential policies

In order to encourage more entrepreneurs and reduce their costs and risks, the government has been lowering the threshold of starting up a business and giving more help, including: allowing phased payment of registration capital, family residences, rented property and temporary commercial buildings as an address; three-year waiver of management, registration and certification fee from the registration day; a government-endorsed small loan up to Rmb50,000 for smallholders (up to Rmb100,000 for university graduates); for people who apply for loans to start a business in less profitable industries, the state pays the loan interest; high-tech enterprises registered in state high-tech parks can enjoy a two-year waiver of corporate income tax, and a 15% reduction afterwards; for qualified small businesses working in less profitable industries, a 20% reduction of corporate income tax is awarded; since January, 2011, smallholders can enjoy Rmb8,000 of tax reduction for three years, covering business tax, urban maintenance and construction tax, education surcharge and personal income tax; in 2011, small enterprises started by university graduates whose taxable revenue is not higher than Rmb30,000 can enjoy a 50% discount of taxable revenue; their corporate income tax rate is 20%; university graduates are no longer required to transfer their household registration back to their homes, but are allowed to register in the place where their universities are located (except for municipalities directly under the State Council); final-year university students can enjoy a government subsidy if they take part in entrepreneurship training. The size of the subsidy depends on the diploma they hold, the results of their entrepreneurial efforts and the grading they receive from training centers.

(2) Platform building

In order to create a good business environment, the government strives to build a platform for entrepreneurs. Measures include: (1) preferential policies are given to entrepreneurial investment and funds to help establish new enterprises; (2) pre-tax deduction of donation to entrepreneurial funds and establishing a guiding fund for entrepreneurial investment; (3) qualified investors are entitled to a 70% deduction of their investment in taxation calculation; (4) opening multiple levels of capital markets to facilitate entrepreneurial efforts, including the Small and Medium-Sized Companies Board in 2004, Pilot System for Stock Transfer Agent in 2006, and Growth Enterprise Market in 2009; continuous efforts are made to improve the technical property transfer market; (5) enhancing information, networking and resource-sharing by creating entrepreneurial clusters, such as regional bases for small start-ups, and incubators, technology parks in universities and entrepreneurial centers for returned overseas students.

(3) Entrepreneurial education

In order to make the workers actively adapt to the diversification of employment patterns, the government has continuously strengthened the education of entrepreneurship and constantly improved vocational training. Governments and government departments at all levels provide entrepreneurial training to university graduates, workers in rural areas who are ready to work in non-agricultural sectors, and returned migrant workers who are going to start their own businesses. Measures include case studies, study trips and conversations with entrepreneurs. In the meantime, universities host courses in areas such as entrepreneurial training, entrepreneurial case studies and investment in mainstream entrepreneurial education. In 2002, the Chinese Ministry of Education identified Tsinghua University, Renmin University of China and Fudan University as pilot key universities for entrepreneurial education. Since 2010, the Ministry of Human Resources and Social Security implemented 'leading plans for university graduate entrepreneurs' that has helped a large number of university graduates start their own companies. In addition, the China Galaxy program provides entrepreneurial and managerial skill training to small and medium-sized company managers. In 2007, China launched a 'torch mentor' plan in which 39 experts and entrepreneurs were invited to assist start-ups and their managers.

4. Government purchase of employment services

Since the late 1990s, the government monopoly of PES was broken and it started to purchase PES instead of supplying it by itself. Encouraged by the central government, a number of local governments introduced the market mechanism to find innovative ways of PES purchase in accordance with laws and regulations concerning government purchase, economic and social development in the area, and the needs of employment promotion. Measures such as funding community service posts and purchasing training capacity have been implemented to boost stronger and more efficient PES supply.

These policies started more than a decade ago when excess labor in rural areas started to transfer to non-agricultural sectors at a faster pace, adding more pressure to urban employment and causing a more acute problem of unemployment. In 2002, the Chinese government issued the *Announcement to Further Enhance Re-employment of Laid-off Workers* to address the problem of the re-employment of former workers of state-owned enterprises who were largely aged over 50 (male) or 40 (female). They were referred to as 'the 40-50s'. Governments started to fund community service jobs for this age group as an effective way to provide more employment opportunities and ease unemployment pressure.

III. Systems, Mechanisms and Policies Adopted by the Chinese Government to Improve the PES System

As the economic system and public employment situation evolved, China enacted a law system on PES with the *Labor Law, Law of the PRC on Employment Contracts* and *Law on Employment Protection* as its core to protect the rights of workers. A series of rules, regulations and policies were formulated to protect their rights and promote employment. Systems such as the minimum wage and collective wage bargaining were established. Micro, small and medium-sized enterprises were encouraged to accept more workers through a system of preferential policies. All these have contributed to long-term social stability and sustained economic development.

1. Minimum wage system

The minimum wage system is a basic system of labor and social security in China. According to the *Labor Law* and *Regulation on the Minimum Wage*, the minimum wage refers to the lowest amount of payment according to the law by the employer to the worker, under the premise that the worker has worked normally[5] in the law-stipulated working time or that arranged by the employment contract signed under the law. Usually, the government regulates two types of minimum wage, monthly and hourly. The monthly

---

[5] 'Working normally' means that the worker, in accordance with a contract signed according to the law, works within the period of time specified by his contract or the law. Workers may receive overtime payment, a stipend due to special working time or working conditions, such as high/low temperature, toxic or hazardous environment, or insurance, benefits required by law and the state, and other non-monetary remuneration paid by the company, including but not limited to meal and accommodation allowances

minimum wage is applicable to full-time workers, while the hourly relates to non-full-time workers.

In general, the minimum wage needs to take into account the cost of living in local urban areas, the consumer price index, social insurance payments by individuals, the housing provident fund, the average wage of workers, the economic development level, employment status and other factors. In determining and adjusting the hourly minimum wage standards, occupational stability, welfare and other factors of non-full-time jobs should also be considered. Minimum wage standards are determined and adjusted by human resources and the labor securities department of province, autonomous region or municipality governments in consultation with trade unions and business associations at the same level, and should be reported to the government for approval. The minimum wage standards are adjusted at least once every two years.

The minimum wage system applies to all enterprises in China, including state-owned enterprises, collective enterprises, foreign-funded enterprises and private enterprises. To date, the people's governments of all provinces, autonomous regions and municipalities directly under the central government in mainland China have promulgated and implemented local minimum wage standards. According to *Several Opinions on Furthering Reforms in Income Distribution* issued in February 2013, China will continue to adjust the minimum wage and, by 2015, in the vast majority of regions, the minimum wage will reach 40% of the average wage of local urban workers and the government will publish separate minimum wage standards for some industries.[6]

2. Wage collective bargaining system

After the reform and opening up, with the rapid development of the non-public economy, labor conflicts have become increasingly prominent. By the early 1990s, many areas started pilot collective bargaining practices followed by central government legislation to regulate collective bargaining. It first incorporated relevant regulations in the *Labor Law* and *Law on Trade Unions*, and then enacted separately in *Regulations on Collective Contract, Interim Regulations on Wage Collective Bargaining*, and *Plans and Guiding Opinions on Conducting Wage Collective Bargaining*. These serve as a legal and policy framework for collective bargaining in China that is aimed at an eventual improvement of the system.

---

[6] http://www.gov.cn/zwgk/2013-02/05/content_2327531.htm (February 17, 2013)

Chapter 5

Agreed by employers and employees   From Xinhua News Agency Zhu Huiqing

According to these laws, rules and regulations, wage collective bargaining refers to the act of signing wage contracts after negotiations between the representatives of employers and employees of enterprises in China on internal affairs concerning wages, such as salary distribution, payment method and income level on an equal footing. The contents of the wage contract may include: the period of the wage agreement; the system of salary distribution, guides on wages and payment methods; the annual average wage level and the adjustment range; the distribution method of the employee's annual salary, benefits and allowances; wage payment method; procedures to alter or annul the contract; termination conditions; liability for breach of contract; and other matters that the sides deem necessary.

At present, with social transformation, industrial upgrading, structural adjustment, rising costs and other conflicts, labor disputes have become more frequent. Collective wage bargaining is an important way to construct harmonious labor relations, which is an important way to safeguard the legitimate rights and interests of workers. Alongside the establishment and improvement of the national wage collective bargaining system, local regulations have been adopted.

As of June 2014, 27 provinces (autonomous regions and municipalities) in China had introduced local regulations or administrative regulations on collective bargaining, 25 provinces (autonomous regions and municipalities) issued a document to carry out collective bargaining, and 29 provinces (autonomous regions and municipalities) had incorporated collective bargaining into the government's performance assessment system.[7]

3. Policies to promote the development of small and medium-sized enterprises (SMEs)

China now has more than 5,000 small and medium-sized enterprises, of which 97% are micro and small enterprises, accounting for 99% of the total number of enterprises. SMEs provide nearly 80% of urban jobs, and are major employers of both laid-off workers from state-owned enterprises and migrant workers from rural areas. SMEs are also major contributors to the employment of college graduates. They have become an important basis to maintain stable and ensure the rapid development of the national economy.

China passed a series of laws, regulations and policies to support SMEs, including the *Law of the PRC on the Promotion of Small and Medium-sized Enterprises, Law on Employment Promotion, Several Opinions on the Further Promotion of Small and Medium-sized Enterprises* and *Opinions on Providing Further Support to Promote the Healthy Development of Micro and Small-sized Enterprises*. Until 2000, preferential policies mostly involved the reduction of income tax. Afterwards, efforts were made to set up a system to promote SME development with Chinese characteristics.

Therefore, major policies were focused on the following aspects:

(1) Fiscal policy

> Set up funds, including an SMEs development fund and targeted fund for SMEs development to support their growth. The SMEs development fund was established in 2012, and a total of Rmb15bn will be channeled in five stages. This fund is mainly used for providing entrepreneurial training and services to SMEs, including a credit guarantee system to support technological advancement, encouraging professionalism and cooperation with large corporations, supporting service agencies to provide SMEs with training and consulting services, boosting the 'going global' strategy of SMEs, and helping SMEs' green initiatives. The targeted fund for SME development was established in 2004 with the aim of supporting the upgrade and transformation of SMEs. The fund will support credit guarantee agencies to provide loan guarantee services to SMEs to enhance

---

[7] http://acftu.workercn.cn/31/201406/11/140611084840457_7.shtml (August 27, 2014)

their competitiveness. In 2014, the fund registered a total value of Rmb11.5bn in four sectors: service system, funding, technological innovation and international partnership.[8]

Promote the development of SMEs through government procurement. In December 2011, the Chinese government promulgated *Interim Regulations on Promoting Small and Medium-sized Enterprises through Government Procurement*. It provides that 30% of the government procurement budget should go to SMEs, and 60% of that should go to micro and small enterprises.[9] In April 2012, the government issued *Opinions on Further Support to the Healthy Development of Small and Medium-sized Enterprises*, which requires that departments in charge of budgeting must ensure that 18% of the government procurement total goes to micro and small enterprises, allow products made by micro- and small-sized enterprises to be bought at a price 6-10% higher than the ceiling set by the government, and 2-3% higher if the products are sold by a consortium of companies in which micro and small enterprises supply more than 30% of all the products.[10]

Reducing government charges and cancelling fees that are not in line with regulations. In November 2011, China's Ministry of Finance and the National Development and Reform Commission decided that SMEs shall be exempted from some administrative, registration and certificate fees for a period of three years starting from 2012 and running to 2014. *Opinions on Further Support to the Healthy Development of Small and Medium-sized Enterprises* requires authorities to streamline and cancel fees charged on companies for administrative approval and compulsory admission.[11]

(2) Taxation policy

Qualified SMEs shall enjoy a 20% deduction in corporate income tax. Micro and small enterprises whose taxable income is equal to or less than Rmb30,000 shall enjoy a 50% deduction of taxable income.

Trade companies and service industries (excluding advertising companies, estate agents, pawnbrokers, sauna, massage parlors and

---

[8] http://news.xinhuanet.com/fortune/2014-05/27/c_126553354.htm (August 27, 2014)
[9] www.gov.cn/zwgk/2011-12/31/content_2034662.htm (February 17, 2013)
[10] www.gov.cn/zwgk/2012-04/26/content_2123937.htm (February 17, 2013)
[11] www.gov.cn/zwgk/2012-04/26/content_2123937.htm (February 17, 2013)

oxygen bars), labor-intensive manufacturing enterprises, and small businesses not located in an industrial park may be entitled to a deduction in business tax, urban maintenance tax and construction tax, education fee and corporate income tax for three years if they employ newly hired qualified unemployed individuals holding a Certificate of Unemployment (with a note showing their qualification), signed contracts lasting longer than one year, and are paying social security for them. For each such person hired, the deduction is Rmb4,000, plus or minus 20% at the discretion of local governments.[12]

Holders of a Certificate of Unemployment (with a note showing their qualification for entrepreneurial taxation deduction) and of an Entrepreneurial Certificate for University Graduates who are self-employed (excluding those working in construction, entertainment, property sales, land-use rights brokerages, advertising companies, estate agents, saunas, massage parlors and oxygen bars), are entitled to a deduction of business tax, tax on urban maintenance and construction, education fee, and individual income tax for three years up to Rmb8,000.[13]

China is also speeding up a pilot policy to levy value-added tax instead of business tax, and constantly raising the threshold of business tax and value-added tax, in order to relieve the burdens on micro and small enterprises.

(3) Credit policy

Establish and improve the credit service system of SMEs to provide loans to qualified SMEs. Priority is given to enterprises working in science and technology that are in line with national industrial policies and have good potential, and micro and small enterprises that are driven by innovation.

---

[12] Those who hold an Employment and Unemployment Registration Certificate (with a clear indication of 'tax policies on enterprise employers' refer to: (a) those laid off from state-owned enterprises; (b) those who are from state-owned enterprises closed down and declared bankrupt and need re-employment; (c) those laid off from collective enterprises established by state-owned enterprises (namely, large collective enterprises established by factories); and (d) other urban registered unemployed persons who are included in the minimum living standard guarantee program and have been unemployed for one year or longer

[13] The holders of Employment and Unemployment Registration Certificate (which includes a clear indication of 'tax policies on self-employment' or is accompanied by a Self-employment Certificate for University and College Graduates) refer to: (a) those who have registered with the public employment service agencies of the human resources and social security departments for unemployment for half a year or longer; (b) those who have registered as unemployed persons from zero-employment families and from urban resident families under the minimum living standard guarantee program and who are of working age; and (c) graduates from colleges and universities within the first year of graduation

Support reemployment projects. Since 2002, a local government-backed guarantee fund was introduced to provide small loan guarantees to laid-off workers of state-owned enterprises. The central government also provides subsidies to this kind of loan so that banks will have more incentive to provide loans to qualified laid-off workers and labor-intensive small enterprises that have hired a large number of these workers. In 2006, it was made clearer that enterprises with a workforce composed of more than 30% of laid-off workers (or 15% for companies hiring more than 100 workers), are eligible to apply for a subsidized loan up to Rmb1m. By 2008, this limit was increased to Rmb2m. Since 2011, the scheme has been widened to include enterprises hiring unemployed university graduates.

Broaden financing channels of SMEs, in particular micro and small enterprises. Support qualified small enterprises to go public or issue debt, They will also be encouraged to make full use of financing resources, such as intellectual property-backed loans, warehouse receipts, operation rights of shops, commercial credit insurance policies, business factoring and pawning.

After many years of hard work, PES in China has been established from scratch, and is playing a positive role in improving people's livelihoods, building a harmonious and moderately prosperous society. For the past decade, social organizations and private entities have joined PES as a supplement to government-oriented PES, enhancing the country's PES capacity. However, PES in China is still at an initial stage and it faces many difficulties, such as: huge employment pressure due to the large population and excess supply of labor; an immature labor market mechanism that lacks exchange among regions, industries, sectors and enterprises; and labor mobility is restricted by the rural-urban dual track system. PES agencies needs to make clear divisions of labor, clarifying who should make the policies and who should supervise, which are public services and which are for business purposes. PES supply in general and the participation of average citizens remain limited. PES management and IT applications require upgrading.

Achieving better employment in a moderately prosperous society was a newly proposed goal at the 18th congress of the CPC. The third plenum of the 18th central committee made new arrangements accordingly. China pledged to "improve systems and mechanisms that boost employment and business startups. We will set up a mechanism that links economic growth and an increase in employment, and improve the responsibility system of the government in promoting employment. We will regulate human resource management, removing all institutional barriers and employment discrimination that affect equal employment, such as the birthplace of a person (city or countryside), industries, social status and gender. We will improve preferential policies for business startups. The aim is to put in place a new mechanism to boost government and private sector support to encourage the general public to start their own businesses. We will improve the public service system for employment that treats both urban and rural areas equally, and build a lifelong vocational training system for workers. We will strengthen the functions of the unemployment insurance system in preventing unemployment and boosting employment, and improve the employment/unemployment monitoring and statistics system. We will innovate the labor relations coordination mechanism, opening up channels for workers to effectively make reasonable appeals."[14]

An improved PES system will yield an improved and more efficient employment system, play a greater role in promoting employment and lifting people's living standards, and contribute more to the full achievement of a moderately prosperous society.

---

[14] http://news.xinhuanet.com/mrdx/2013-11/16/c_132892941.htm (December 3, 2013)

Chapter 6

China's Health Care System Reform

Good health is fundamental to an individual's survival and development, and also a basic requirement and final goal of economic development and social advancement. Having a sound health care system concerns the health and wellbeing of the people. China's constitution provides that the state develops medical and health care, including both modern and traditional medicine to protect the health of the people. The Chinese government attaches great importance to health care, and has listed 'having a sound health care system' as one of the goals of a moderately prosperous society. It strives to improve the system steadily and ensure that all 1.3bn Chinese can enjoy basic health care.

I. Basic Facts and Figures about China's Health Care System

After the foundation of the People's Republic, especially after the reform and opening up, China has made remarkable achievements in medical and health undertakings.

1. People's overall health has improved, ranking prominently in developing countries. Average life expectancy in China increased from 35 in 1949 to 74.8 in 2010 (see chart 1); infant mortality dropped from 200 per 1,000 to 12.1 per 1,000 (see chart 2); maternal mortality fell from 1,500 per 100,000 to 26 (see chart 3), lower than the world average of 40. The gap between urban and rural areas was significantly reduced. China achieved the UN Millennium Development goals ahead of schedule.

2. Health care resources increased. By the end of 2012, China had 950,000 medical institutions, including 23,000 hospitals and 91,300 grassroots-level health institutions. For every 10,000 people, there are 42.3 hospital beds, 19 registered (assistant) practitioners and 18 registered nurses.

Chart 1 Average Expected Age

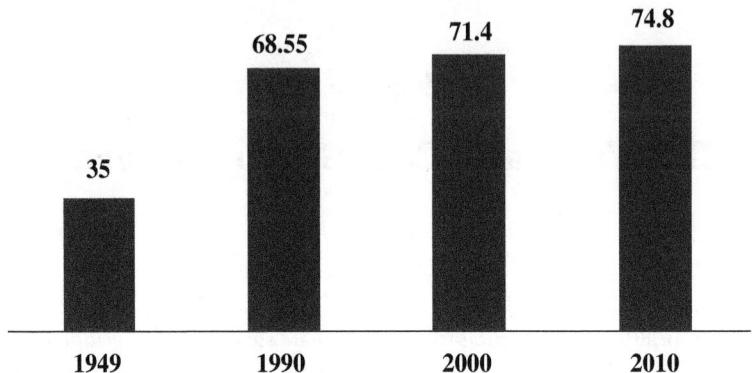

Chart 2 Infant Mortality Rate(‰)

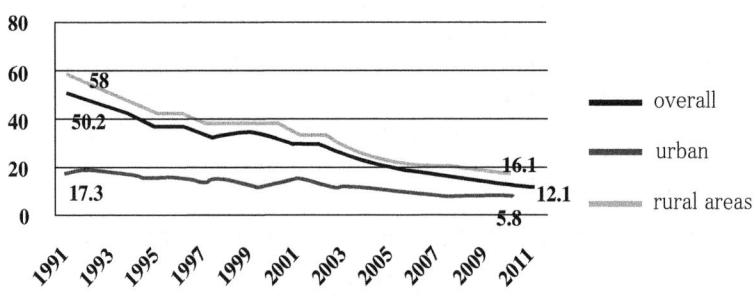

Source: China Statistical Yearbooks, 1990-2011

Chart 3 Maternal Mortality Rate(1/100 thousand)

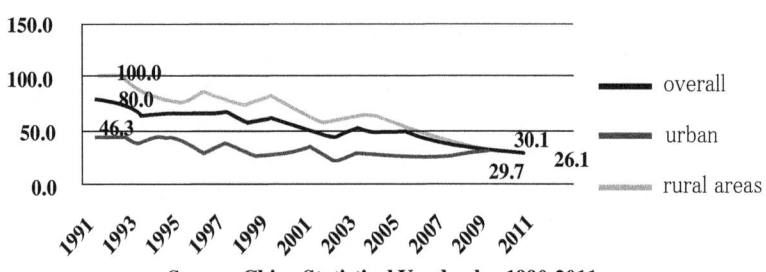

Source: China Statistical Yearbooks, 1990-2011

3. Building the world's largest medical insurance network. By the end of 2012, basic medical insurance for urban workers, urban residents' basic medical insurance and the new rural cooperative medical insurance registered more than 1.3bn participants in total, covering more than 95% of the entire population. The new rural cooperative medical insurance system has 805m participants, covering 98.3% of the qualified population, and has processed 1.745bn claims. The development gap in the health care system between urban and rural areas has gradually narrowed. In 2003, 55% of the urban population had basic medical insurance, outnumbering the proportion in rural areas, which stood at 21% of the rural population. In 2012, the two figures increased to 89% and 98% respectively, showing that the rural coverage was now higher than that in urban areas.

4. The structure of health care financing has been optimized, the burden on residents has been reduced and the fairness of financing has been improved. In China, health care funding has three main channels: government input, social insurance and personal expenditure. In 2012, the proportion of personal health expenditure in China's total health expenditure dropped from 59.97% in 2001 to 34.4%, while government expenditure and social insurance increased from 15.9% and 24.1% to 30% and 35.6%, respectively.

Despite the headway made in China's medical and health undertakings, many difficulties remain. With the progress of industrialization, urbanization and population ageing, the country faces the double threat of infectious disease and chronic disease that leads to increased demands on health care services. In the meantime, China continues to faces a shortage of high quality medical resources and imbalanced distribution. In order to adapt to new developments, the government keeps improving the medical and health care system after assessing the needs and drawing lessons from past experience.

II. China's Medical and Health Care System Reform

Health care reform is challenging all over the world. In recent years, many countries have been promoting health care reform, but most of them have encountered many difficulties. China is a developing country with a large population, low per-capita income level, and a big development gap between urban and rural areas. Promoting health care reform in China is a highly complicated and difficult task. After taking into account the country's basic conditions and development levels and drawing lessons from past international experience, the government has made useful experiments in improving the health care and medical system with Chinese characteristics. The reform also features particularities of China's economic development. It can be divided into the following three stages.

1. The planned economy period: government-dominant model

During the planned economy period, the government organized and managed medical services, and ensured medical and health input through national plans. Public hospitals directly established by the government constituted the main force of providing medical services. Revenues from services were not linked to the income of medical institutions and professionals.

Medical and health care supply had the following features: first, special attention was given to build grassroots-level medical institutions in urban and rural areas, thus improving the availability of medical and health care services. Second, prevention was underscored. A public health system that included sanitation and anti-epidemic services, maternity and child care, local disease control network and hygiene inspection at national borders was established. Good preventive work reduced the risks and cost of medical care. Third, hospitals were directly organized and managed by the government, and medical resources were allocated by the government through planning. The government, state-owned enterprises and collective economic organizations in rural areas covered the vast majority of medical expenses, even those of family members of workers could be partly reimbursed. This free model ensured that all people, including those in economic difficulty, could have access to medical care, which featured fairness in medical care and health care. However, there were problems, including low skill levels, and over-stringent government planning that hindered the development of medical institutions and professionals. As the economy grew and personal income improved, people developed higher and more diverse demands on medical care that required a diversified supply of health care service.

In general terms, the government-led model was in line with the country's prevailing economic development and played a positive role. Effective institutional arrangements made it possible for China to use only 3% of GDP to basically satisfy the health care needs of all society members. The health of the nation was improving rapidly. A number of health indicators reached the level of middle-income countries, while the Chinese economy was at a lower level. Some foreign institutions praised this model as an example for developing countries.

2. The socialist market economy period: market-oriented model

As economic reforms progressed, lessons learned were applied to medical care and health care services. The government wanted to rely on market forces to address the situation. China's medical and health care system changed considerably compared with the planned economy years: first, multiple ownership was introduced to medical institutions; second, government spending on medical institutions was reduced to encourage the market-oriented management of medical institutions, including public hospitals, and a move towards economic independence; third, administrative responsibility of medical care and health care services was transferred largely to local governments that led to imbalanced service levels and accessibility among regions, and between urban and rural areas.

In this period, the market injected new vitality into the field of medical care and health care. Through market competition, the supply level of health care services was obviously increased, the number of medical institutions, medical professionals and beds was greatly increased, the technical level of medical service, efficiency and work morale of medical institutions and professionals improved. Market-oriented reform has changed the shortage of medical and health care resources and supply that suffered during the first years of the People's Republic.

However, over-marketization and commercialization also had drawbacks. First, people's medical expenditure was increased and some were reduced to poverty due to medical spending. After abolishing the free health care system, the social security and medical insurance systems were not established immediately, which meant that 90% of the population were not covered by medical insurance. They needed to pay all expenses. Second, social fairness, efficiency and performance of medical institutions was reduced. In 2000, China ranked 188 out of 191 member states in a World Health Organization (WHO) survey of fairness in medical resources distribution, and at 144 in terms of overall performance and efficiency. China responded poorly to the 2003 SARS crisis, causing loss of human life and property and disrupting the national economy.

The market-oriented reforms made it clear that health care cannot rely fully on the market. Health care services are a part of public services. Without government intervention, they will go off track.

3. Combining market-oriented reform and government steering in improving the new type of medical and health care services

China started a new round of medical care and health care reform in 2009 after drawing lessons from past experience. The State Council issued *Opinion on Deepening Institutional Reform in Medical and Health Care System* (hereinafter referred to as the Opinion) and *Announcement to Publish Key Plans for Institutional Reform in the Medical and Health Care System in the Near Future (2009-2011)*. These documents proposed one objective, four systems, five major reform programs and eight supportive measures. The objective is to build a basic health care system that universally covers all urban and rural residents to provide safe, effective, convenient and affordable services. The four systems are a public hygiene and sanitation service system, health care system, medical insurance system and medicine supply system that jointly serve as pillars to China's basic health care system. The five reform programs include: (1) speeding up the construction of a basic medical insurance system; (2) putting in place a national essential drug system; (3) improving the grassroots health care service system; (4) improving equal access to basic public hygiene and sanitation services; (5) promoting reforms in public hospitals. The eight measures cover management, operation, input, pricing, supervision, technology research and talent cultivation institutions, IT application, and legislation of medical care and health care in China to support the effective execution of the reform.

Compared with previous health care reform, this new reform has the following features:

First of all, it has returned to underscore public interest. The Opinion gave a blueprint for the reform by 2020, and emphasized that basic medical care and health care services comprise part of China's public services system to secure the basic needs of the people to health care and achieve the goal of universal coverage. This has embodied the idea of putting people first and serving the people, and was a conclusion after a deep analysis of the country's basic conditions and the relationship between good health and economic and social development. The government has underscored the need to provide an institutional guarantee to universal coverage of basic medical care and health care services regardless of a resident's place of residence, ethnicity, age, sex, profession and income level. It shows that the party and the government aim to serve the people. By underscoring universal coverage, the Opinion is putting more weight on the public good dimension of medical and health care services, recognizing that they constitute a part of each citizen's fundamental rights. And by underscoring the word 'basic', the Opinion is putting equal weight on explaining that services should be proportionate to China's economic and social development in the primary stage of socialism, and should be affordable to the country, society and individuals. Due to differences in their social system and development level, countries provide medical and health care services at different levels with different coverage. China remains a developing country with a large population and weak economic foundation, which determines that the rationale to development in health care must highlight low level, wide coverage, securing basic needs, gradual improvement and development'. It also made clear that China's medical and health care system include the following services: disease control and prevention, health education, maternity and child care, mental health care, emergency response, blood donation and supply, medical supervision, family planning, disease diagnosis, cure and rehabilitation.

Second, the new reform stresses the combination of market-oriented reform and government steering. On one hand, the government must shoulder its due responsibility in building the basic medical and health care system and maintain its leading role in providing services. It must address the problem of fairness. The new reform has clear requirements on government input, demanding a gradual increase in the proportion of government spending in overall health care expenditure to substantially reduce the spending of individuals. It also requires the government to enhance supervision and promote access to hygiene and sanitation and health care services. On the other hand, it also underscores the role of the market under the supervision of the government. The government should guide and regulate private capital to invest in medical and health care to increase supply according to the many kinds of needs of the people. The aim is to improve the structure of medical and health care service supply to provide satisfactory services to the people. The market largely addresses the question of efficiency.

Third, the new reform is more transparent and open in the decision-making process, with enhanced public participation. In September 2006, China set up a reform coordination group consisting of 11 relevant ministries and commissions with the director of the National Development and Reform Commission and the health minister as joint directors. By the end of October, the commission and the Ministry of Health released an online consultation to the public and it collected more than 5,000 responses. In 2007, the coordination group invited for the first time international organizations and foreign consulting firms, such as the World Bank, the WHO, and Mckinsey & Co to conduct research programs on overall path and framework design for China's medical care, health care and medicine system. Domestic institutions, such as the Development Research Centre of the State Council, Peking University, Fudan University and Beijing Normal University were commissioned with same research. This was aimed at hearing a broad range of opinions from think-tanks. A draft version of the Opinion was released online on October 14, 2008 for public consultation. The National Bureau on Health Care Reform received 35,929 suggestions, as a result of which 190 major changes were made to the draft that resulted in the 2009 final version of the Opinion.

III. Measures Taken by the Chinese Government to Ensure Universal Access to Basic Health Care Services

The key to ensuring universal access to basic health care services is to build a basic health care system that includes a public hygiene and sanitation service system, health care system, medical insurance system and medicine supply system.

1. Establishing a basic public hygiene and sanitation service system

China vigorously promotes the construction of a public hygiene and sanitation service system that secures basic services with a strong grassroots presence and institutions. After identifying basic and major items, equal access to services was largely improved, and the capacity to respond to emergencies enhanced. The system has achieved good results.

(1) Strengthening the disease prevention system

China has four levels of disease prevention and control institutions: national, provincial, city and county. Health care centers in rural towns and health service units in villages, all levels of hospitals and medical institutions in urban areas also constitute part of the system. Currently, 100% of disease prevention and control institutions, 98% of medical institutions at levels higher than county level, and 87% of health care centers in rural towns have connected to the online pandemic and public health emergency report system. Quality and timeliness are improving every year.

(2) Improving the response mechanism to public health emergencies

After the SARS epidemic, the Central Committee of the CPC and the State

Chapter 6

Council underscored the necessity to establish a response mechanism to public health emergencies. On May 7, 2003, the State Council reviewed and adopted the *Regulation on Response to Public Health Emergencies*, and established a decision-making and leading system at the national, provincial and city levels.

(3) Improving equal access to public health services

According to the new reform plan, China now provides 42 services in 11 types of basic health services, including citizen's health records, health education, disease prevention and vaccination, child care, maternity care, elderly care, health management for people with chronic diseases, management of major mental diseases, communicable diseases, reporting and responding to public health emergencies, supervision of health care services. The government promulgated *National Service Standards of Public Health Services (2009)*, setting annual per capita spending at Rmb15, which was increased to Rmb25 in 2011 and Rmb30 in 2013. These measures have secured fairness in China's health care system as the number of service items increases and coverage expands.

2 Improving basic medical and health care services

Medical and health care services in China features mutual linkage between grassroots-level medical institutions and higher-level hospitals, equal emphasis of Chinese traditional medicine and western medical science, and the co-existence of public and private medical institutions.

(1) Strengthening the medical service system at the grassroots level

China has equipped most villages with health care units, towns with health care centers, counties with qualified hospitals, and communities with health services stations. The central government invested Rmb47.15bn from 2009 to 2011 to support the building of medical institutions at grassroots levels, according a 2012 report by the Information Office of the State Council. Increased government input has led to an enhanced service system in rural villages and urban communities, which in turn secured improved accessibility. As detailed in the *White Paper on Medical and Health Services in China*, preferential policies have been made to train and introduce competent personnel for rural and community health care. A system of general practitioners (medical workers with sufficient knowledge in all branches of medicine) has been established, under which general practitioners are trained in the regular way; grassroots medical and health care workers are enrolled in training courses for upgrading them to general practitioners; and medical students are specially trained for the needs of central and western urban areas, for which they do not have to pay tuition fees. A project, known as '10,000 doctors extending support to rural medical care' has been launched. All these factors have improved the level of services in county-level hospitals and township-level health care centers both in terms of management and medical skills.

(2) Promoting reform in public hospitals

The State Council's *Opinion on Pilot Reform Programs in Public Hospitals* was published in February 2010, asking for "the promotion of institutional and mechanical innovations to bolster working morale of medical professionals and make public hospitals more efficient; an emphasis on public good in public hospitals and the top priority should be safeguarding people's health; separation of administrative and technical responsibilities, supervision and management, service and drug supply, pro-profit and non-profit services." Sixteen cities were chosen as pilot areas to be the first adopters of the reform. Before the reform, as government input shrank, hospital revenues depended largely on selling drugs. After the reform, this model was eliminated. In the meantime, hospital supervision and management were transferred to different government departments in order to streamline decision-making. Doctors and hospitals started to put patients first and gave up previous practices such as issuing expensive prescriptions, asking for unnecessary checks and excessive medical care.

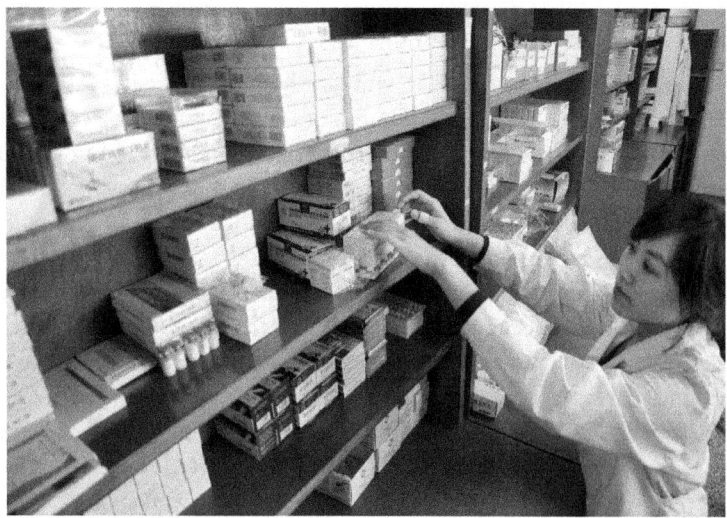

(3) Promoting the diversification of medical institutions

The fundamental principle and direction of China's medical and health reform is to insist on the leading role of public institutions, and encourage the development of non-public institutions to shape a diversified landscape in the industry. The State Council approved the *Report for Permission for Individuals to Open Medical Institutions* by the Ministry of Health, thus ending state monopoly in this area and allowing multiple ownership to be introduced. In 2010, the State Council issued *Opinion on Further Encouraging and Guiding Private Capital to Open Medical Institutions*, stated the importance of having non-public medical institutions and provided institutional guarantees for entrepreneurs. The third plenum of the 18th Central Committee of the CPC stated in its *Decision of the CCCPC on Some Major Issues Concerning Comprehensively Deepening the Reform*: "We will encourage private funds to flow to medical services, first supporting them to flow to not-for-profit medical institutions. We will allow private funds to invest directly in services that are short of resources or to meet diverse demands, and to participate in the reform and restructuring of public hospitals in various forms."

(4) Constantly strengthening the traditional Chinese medicine service system

Traditional Chinese medicine (TCM) has a long history. It is a branch of medical science that has arisen from the long-lasting practice of curing disease by the Chinese people. Since the foundation of the People's Republic, the CPC and the State Council put a strong emphasis on TCM. In the State Council's 2009 *Opinions on Supporting and Promoting Traditional Chinese Medicine*, it asks that equal weight is given to TCM and western medical science. It went on to say that the government should strive to improve the service system and training of practitioners of TCM and help TCM to have a greater international presence. By 2012, 68.8% of community health care centers, 24.4% of community health care stations, 60% of township health care centers and 32.4% of village health care units provided TCM services.

3. Establishing a national essential drug system

According to the definition of the World Health Organization in 1999, essential drugs refer to those that meet the health care needs of the majority of the population and can be supplied at any time in sufficient quantities and appropriate dosage forms with affordable prices for individuals and communities. In order to achieve full coverage of basic medical and health care services, secure basic medical treatment for most patients, and reduce high medical expenditure caused by high drug prices, China has established and is constantly improving the national essential drug system.

The Ministry of Health and eight other authorities issued on August 18, 2009 the *National Catalog of Essential Drugs* after consulting international practices, combing requirements of grassroots medical institutions and common usage of drugs in hospitals that includes 307 items. It contains drugs for both curing diseases and disease prevention, featuring safety and convenience, and giving equal weight to TCM and western medicine. It largely includes basic drugs that are the first choice for doctors. In principle, the catalogue should be revised every three years. All essential drugs will be put under government price control. In counties, cities and city districts where the national essential drug system applies, grassroots-level medical institutions sponsored by the state sell drugs at government-set prices. All essential drugs are included in the *Catalog of Government Reimbursement of Drugs*, and enjoy higher rates of reimbursement than non-essential drugs. The system helps to reduce expenditure and regulate a practitioner's everyday service.

4. Improving the basic medical insurance system

Article 45 of *Constitution of the PRC* provides that "citizens of the PRC have the right to material assistance from the state and society when they are old, ill or disabled. The state develops the social insurance, social relief and medical and health services that are required to enable citizens to enjoy this right." Establishing and improving a universal medical insurance system is an important measure to safeguard every citizen's right to medical and health care and reduce the economic risks from disease.

Since the reform and opening up, the Chinese government has made a series of major decisions and actively promoted the reform of the basic medical insurance system. The basic principle, after considering the country's basic conditions, is stated as "wide coverage to secure basic needs with multiple levels for sustainable development". The government took pilot programs in some communities and then expanded them to the entire country. It also gradually improved financing and assurance levels alongside economic development to reduce the discrepancy of benefits enjoyed by different groups.

China has built the world's largest basic medical insurance system, covering more than 1.3bn people. It now has universal coverage of medical insurance. In China, the basic medical insurance for urban workers, basic medical insurance for urban residents and the new rural cooperative medical insurance system, known as *xinnonghe*, are the three pillars of the basic medical insurance system. The medical aid system for urban and rural residents, supplementary medical insurance and commercial health insurance are complements to the system.

(1) Basic medical insurance for urban workers

By the end of 1998, China began to introduce reforms to transfer the free health care system as a part of state-owned enterprise welfare into the social insurance system. By the end of 2012, the basic medical insurance for urban workers registered 260m participants, which meant it covered all urban workers. The principal to the insurance is paid jointly by the employee and employer.

(2) *Xinnonghe*

Pilot programs were introduced in 2003 followed by nationwide implementation in 2008. By the end of 2012, there were 805m registered participants. The *xinnonghe* is a system of basic medical insurance designed for rural residents sponsored mainly by the government to pay for the cost of in-patient services. Governments at all levels provide participants with subsidies.

(3) The medical aid system for urban and rural residents

The rural and urban system was established in 2003 and 2005 respectively. The system is funded by the government to help people in both areas with economic difficulties who are unable to afford payments to basic medical insurance so that they will be included in the basic medical insurance systems. Aid is mainly provided to people with low incomes who suffer from poverty due to ill health and other reasons. Government funding apart, the system also accepted private donations. In 2012, 80.51m claims were processed, of which 74% came from rural residents. Total spending in 2012 was Rmb20.38bn.

(4) Basic medical insurance for urban residents

A pilot program started in 2007 to incorporate non-working students, children and the elderly in rural areas in the basic medical insurance for urban residents, followed by national implementation in 2009. By the end of 2012, 270m people had joined. Local governments decide the payment according to local economic development and the principle of establishing a share of funding between families and the state. The threshold is generally low.

IV. International Health Care Cooperation by the Chinese Government

China has been actively involved in global health undertakings by wide participation in multilateral and bilateral cooperation and joining forces with intergovernmental and civil society partners in the health care field. It plays an active role in major health initiatives of the international community and organizations.

China has always attached great importance to international health aid. In 1963, despite serious difficulties in the domestic economy, China organized the best professionals to send its first medical aid team to Algeria. This marked the first step in China's medical assistance to Africa. By June 2013, China had sent a total of 230,000 medical professional to 66 countries and territories in Asia, Africa, Latin America, Europe and Oceania. More than 11,000 of them are currently working in 113 medical stations in 49 countries and territories, of whom 95% have grade 2-3 professional titles. They brought with them TCM skills, such as acupuncture and massage, along with modern medicine. These skills helped foreign countries, including those in Africa, cure difficult and complicated cases. Since 2010, short-term medical teams have been dispatched to Yemen, Botswana and Algeria to provide free surgery to cataract patients. More than 1,000 successful surgeries have been performed. Chinese professional provide training to local medical practitioners by giving lectures, on-site teaching and technology consultation. China donates medicine and medical equipment to recipient countries, sends medical missions and has constructed hundreds of hospitals and medical centers free of charge. These medical professionals are warmly welcomed because of their skills, high morale and strong morality. About 900 of them have been awarded medals issued by foreign countries. Around 50 of them sacrificed their lives in the receiving counties. They have helped host countries to improve health care by improving skills and infrastructure.

The Chinese government is determined to establish a basic medical and health care system covering all urban and rural residents by 2020 to secure basic medical and health care services for all. To this end, China will continue to deepen reform, comprehensively develop health care undertakings to better safeguard, protect and improve the health of all residents. It will continue to actively participate in global health cooperation to work with all parties in making greater efforts to improve global health.

Chapter 7

China's Basic Elderly Care Reform

Chinese society is ageing rapidly and faces greater pressure to provide elderly care. The country's reproduction model changed in a relatively short period of time and now features low birth, mortality and natural growth rates. That has caused a rapid increase in the proportion of older people in the population. This chapter begins with an introduction to China's system of basic elderly care, then focuses on the family support model, the country's modern system of elderly care, and state measures to improve the old-age insurance system in rural areas. This chapter also addresses new challenges arising from having an ageing population, and introduces policies to build a fairer and more sustainable social security system.

I. Basic Elderly Care in China

The modern elderly care system has been formed gradually since the foundation of the People's Republic. After 1949, the state gave priority to the development of industry, especially modern industries, and thus the industrial population continued to expand. The socialization of mass production activities also promoted the socialization of human lifestyles, and it appeared necessary to establish a new social elderly care system to ensure social stability and productivity. This gave birth to a modern elderly care system compatible to the nation's conditions.

In 1997, the Chinese government formulated *Decision on Establishing a Unified Basic Old-age Insurance System for Employees of Enterprises*, and began to establish a unified basic old-age insurance system for urban workers, which was a big leap forward in promoting modern elderly care. This system was supported both by a national security package[15] and personal accounts,

---

[15] An umbrella fund into which many subordinate funds channel their assets. In the Chinese pension system, the national security package is managed by the government and funded by employers

which were funded by the employer and individual contributions, as well as government subsidies. Enterprises and their employees must fulfill their obligations to pay. In 2011, pilot programs were launched for old-age insurance to cover all residents in urban areas, expanding coverage to those who were not working at the time. That marked the establishment of the old-age social security system for urban residents.

> **Example:**
>
> **Social Insurance Law Of the PRC**
>
> (Adopted at the 17th meeting of the Standing Committee of the 11th National People's Congress on October 28, 2010)
>
> (1) Main obligations of the parties. Workers shall participate in basic pension insurance and basic pension insurance premiums shall be paid jointly by the employing entities and the workers.
>
> Sole proprietors who are not employed, non-full time practitioners and other workers in flexible employment who have not participated in the basic pension insurance in the employing entities may participate in basic pension insurance and pay the basic pension insurance premiums on their own.
>
> Measures for the pension insurance of civil servants and staff governed by civil servant laws shall be prescribed by the State Council.
>
> (2) Main rights of the parties. An individual participating in basic pension insurance may collect a monthly basic pension if the cumulative premium payment period reaches 15 years at the time the individual reaches the statutory retirement age.
>
> If the cumulative premium payment period is less than 15 years at the time the individual participating in basic pension insurance reaches the statutory retirement age, he/she may continue to pay the premium until the cumulative premium payment period reaches 15 years and then collect the basic pension on a monthly basis. Alternatively, he/she may transfer to the new rural social pension insurance or the social pension insurance for urban residents and enjoy the corresponding pension insurance benefits in accordance with the provisions of the State Council.

1. China has established a basic elderly care system with Chinese characteristics that boosts 'low starting point and wide coverage'. This is the result of combining Chinese realities with global practices. Based on its prevailing level of economic development, China devised a system of social security that is managed and regulated by the state and provides low-level basic coverage that will improve as the economy grows, with the ultimate goal of universal service. Since the first half of 2012, the State Council started to implement a new social security system in rural areas and old-age social insurance for urban residents. Although progress has been made, China still has much to do to achieving universal coverage of old-age care.

2. China's elderly care system is supported by the troika of individual contribution, social participation and government mandate. The required funds are paid for jointly by the state, enterprises and individuals. The system provides wide and mutual social support to citizens and has a strong influence in civil society. By the end of September 2012, old-age social security insurance registered a total of 700m participants in urban and rural areas. The state enacted a law to mandate compulsory participation. In 2010, the NPC passed *Social Insurance Law of the PRC*, which came into effect on July 1, 2011.

3. China's elderly care system is divided into two models, one paid for and the other unpaid. The former system is further classified into three categories: basic social old-age insurance, enterprise annuity and commercial life insurance. The target of this system is the working community in urban areas. The non-paid model refers to social relief and family-supported elderly care. The main beneficiaries of this model are elderly people with economic difficulties. It merits special attention that the traditional family-supported elderly care system in China remains effective.

II. Family-supported Elderly Care System in China

This is the mainstream model of elderly care in China and means that the family is primarily responsible for supporting the elderly, paying for their expenses no matter whether they continue to live at home or go to a nursing home. In ancient and modern times, the family is considered the basic unit of production and everyday life, and therefore should be primarily responsible for supporting the elderly. There are three main reasons:

1. China is an agricultural country with a long history, and it is common in agricultural civilizations to revere the elderly. The family is the basic unit of agricultural production. A family is a small society in which the husband and wife take different roles and is different from the family model under mass social production and labor division in Europe. The elderly, though unable to continue working on the land, are highly respected and adored by the family members because of their rich experience. Therefore, care for the elderly is usually a family responsibility.

2. The family plays a unique role in one's life. Chinese society attaches importance to one's family and working affiliation; the former is far more important as it is believed that people spend more time with family members. Therefore, working hard and having a harmonious family become guarantees for good elderly care.

3. It is a part of Chinese culture to save money to prepare for elderly care. Filial piety is essential to the traditional Confucian value sets of the Chinese that underscores family. Traditionally, children have an obligation to support their parents economically and, in turn, parents will also save much to prepare for their own retirement. In conclusion, the family-supported model is rooted in China's traditional production model, living patterns and culture, and it naturally comprises an important part of China's elderly care system.

III. Modern Social Elderly Care Model in China

The report of the 18th National Congress of the CPC pointed out with special emphasis that a social security system that provides full coverage to both urban and rural residents – featuring universal coverage, basic services, multi-level supply and sustainability, and bolstering fairness, adaptability and mobility, and sustainability – must be put in place. After years of development, China now has a complicated elderly care insurance system that has seven tracks, according to researcher Tang Jun of the Research Centre for Social Policies, China Academy of Social Sciences, comprising those for state functionaries, state-sponsored institutions, servicemen, enterprise employers, farmers, urban residents and migrant workers. The seven tracks can be classified into five types, and three systems. The five types are: (1) elderly care insurance for government departments and state-sponsored institutions; (2) new social elderly care insurance in rural areas (*xinnongbao*); (3) basic elderly care insurance for enterprise employers in urban areas; (4) elderly care insurance for urban residents (*chengjubao*); (5) insurance for residents in urban and rural areas (*chengxiangjubao*), which is a reform result of combining *xinnongbao* and *chengjubao*. The three major systems are: (1) an insurance system for government departments and state-sponsored institutions; (2) for rural residents; (3) for urban employers and residents.

(1) Elderly care insurance for government departments and state-sponsored institutions

After taking account of historical practices in China and the policies of foreign governments, civil servants were given better pensions to attract highly qualified candidates. The current system in based on the pay-as-you-go (PAYG) principle, meaning that worker contributions and taxes are used to finance the pensions of current pensioners. Pensions are calculated proportionate to the basic salary received by the retiree at the last month of his or her service. The adjustment rate is linked to changes applied to the income of in-service personnel.[16] The main objective is to attract top talent to work in the public sector, and the pension is also seen as a compensation for the relatively low incomes while they are in service. Their pension is fully covered by state funding or by the institution they serve, and is based on the retiree's income, adjusted according to the length of service. This system is not unique to China, yet recently there have been increasing demands calling for convergence of this system with the social basic elderly care insurance.

(2) *Xinnongbao*

For the first 40 years after 1949, family-supported elderly care was the main system in rural areas. In the early 1990s, pilot programs were launched in some rural areas. Changes were made due to the complicated and distinctive conditions in different areas. It was not until 2009 that the state started to implement *xinnongbao*, followed by national implementation in all counties in the first half of 2012. Provinces and autonomous regions have different standards, which will be introduced in following sections.

(3) *Chengjubao*

This system covers working and non-working residents in urban areas. Those who are not working are required to pay basic elderly care insurance fees according to government regulations into the national security package and personal account. Working people enjoy both basic pension and enterprise

---

[16] Tong Limin.*Social Work for the Elderly* [M] East China University of Science and Technology Press. 2006, page 135

annuity, also known as supplementary elderly care insurance for enterprises. The basic pension is paid jointly by the national security package and individual contributions to the personal account. The state gives policy support and acts as payer of last resort. After 1997, the government decided to curb payments to the national security package to around one-fifth of an enterprise's total payroll, and 8% to personal accounts. The supplementary elderly care insurance for enterprises was renamed 'enterprise annuities' in 2004, which are supplementary retirement plans set up by enterprises for their employees. The funding to annuities can either be paid entirely by the employer, or jointly by the employer and employee according to a negotiated ratio. This serves as an important supplement to state elderly care systems, and a remarkable step forward towards a diversified elderly care system.

IV. Measures to Improve the Rural Elderly Care Insurance System

The basic elderly care insurance system in rural areas is an influential part of China's rural social security system as well as the country's general social security system. It relates to the quality of life of rural inhabitants and migrant workers, who account for half of the country's population. With the population movement in rural areas caused by urbanization and the changes in family and society structure in rural areas, elderly care is increasingly becoming a serious problem that demands the improvement of the basic elderly care insurance system in rural areas.

1. Evolution of the elderly care system for rural residents

In the early days of the People's Republic, China experienced a period of economic difficulty and, in order to speed up industrialization, the state prioritized the allocation of resources to urban areas and suppressed agricultural product prices to support urban development. Social security, including elderly care in rural areas, was long seen as a secondary problem. It was given more emphasis only after rural reforms following the start of the household responsibility system.

Pioneering implementation of new social elderly care insurance in rural areas (*xinnongbao*) was started in 2009. The Ministry of Human Resources and Social Security explains that the *xinnongbao* has two distinctive features: (1) funding – the *xinnongbao* is jointly funded by individual payment, subsidies from villages and government allowances, while in the past, rural residents were required to pay for their own elderly care; (2) pension payment structure – under *xinnongbao*, the pension a retired farmer receives is divided into two parts: a basic pension, which is 100% guaranteed by the state fund; and a phased withdrawal of personal deposits from individual accounts.

2. Status quo of elderly care in rural areas

As China runs a dual-track governance system in rural and urban areas, and economic development in urban and rural areas is imbalanced, different elderly care systems were created. The basic social elderly care system in rural areas is relatively young, with few commercial life insurance products targeted at rural areas. The traditional elderly care model in rural areas is collapsing at the same time due to the migration of young, working-age farmers to the cities and the reduced size of rural families due to the one-child policy. The sixth national census showed that the average number of per household residents dropped from 3.44 in 2000 to 3.1 in 2010. That means the rural population is in urgent need of a modern social security system.

3. Laws, regulations and policies governing elderly care in rural areas

Articles 20 and 21 of the *Social Insurance Law of the PRC* adopted on October 28, 2010 provide that: "The state shall establish and improve the new rural social insurance of the old-age pension. The new rural social insurance of the old-age pension shall be a combination of individual contributions, collective subsidies and government allowances. The benefits of the new rural social insurance of the old-age pension shall consist of base pensions and individual account benefits. A rural resident who is a member of the new rural social insurance of the old-age pension shall receive benefits of the new rural social insurance of the old-age pension on a monthly basis when the member satisfies the conditions set by the state." These are the principles according to which *xinnongbao* was formulated.

The basic principle of *xinnongbao* is described as 'securing basic needs and ensuring a flexible and sustainable system with wide coverage'. First of all, pension standards should be in line with the economic development and affordability of rural residents and the government. This means that, at the beginning, payment will be kept at a low level, meeting the actual consumption needs in rural areas. Second, the obligation to pay for the pension fund is taken jointly by the government, villages (collective economic organizations) and individuals. Third, rural residents are encouraged to participate in the system under government guidance and based on voluntary choices. The laws provides that rural residents who take part in *xinnongbao* and have paid in for a required minimum period of time, shall draw the basic pension after 60.

> **Example:**
>
> **New Type of Elderly Care Insurance in Jinzhou**
>
> The people's government of Liaoning province has announced the release of a working plan for Jinzhou city on the launch of new social elderly care insurance in rural areas, and it will be effective on July 1, 2011. Rural residents who are not involved in urban elderly care insurance and are older than 16 can voluntarily take part in *xinnongbao* at their household registration place. The insurance is divided into two parts: a basic pension of Rmb55 per person per month, and an individual account, which can be withdrawn monthly after being divided by 139. Participants must choose from five levels of insurance package, which offer basic pensions ranging from Rmb100 to Rmb500 per month, which they are entitled to claim for the rest of their lives.

V. Elderly Care Challenges that an Ageing China Faces

Chinese society is rapidly ageing and faces mounting pressure to provide elderly care. China's reproduction model changed in a relatively short period of time and now features low birth, mortality and natural growth rates. That has caused a rapid increase in the proportion of older people in the population. The situation in megacities such as Shanghai is even worse: 23% of its population are over 60, nearly twice the national average.

1. Basic characteristics of an ageing China

According to internationally accepted standards, a society is ageing when more than 7% of the total population is aged 65 and over, or more than 10% are 60 and over. According to the sixth census, China's population composition was as follows: 0-14, 16.60%; 15-59, 70.14%, over 60, 13.26%, and over 65, 8.87%. Chinese society therefore is clearly ageing with two prominent characteristics: (1) a rapidly ageing society – 170m people aged 60 and over, and it is estimated that this figure will continue to grow at an annual average rate of 4% for four decades, greatly outpacing the annual average growth rate of the total population, which stands at 1.68% and, (2) society is not well off enough to cope with this pace. The population in most developed countries started to age after economic take-off and industrialization. When the process started, per capita GDP stood at around US$7,000. However, Chinese society is ageing while income levels remain low, with per capita GDP standing at around half of that of developed countries.

2. New challenges brought by an ageing population to elderly care insurance

It will be a long-term strategic task for China to respond proactively to these new challenges. In the meantime, when the population is rapidly ageing, industrialization, urbanization and modernization are advancing, with pressure coming from large development gaps among rural and urban areas and regions, and a huge income gap. Changes in population structure have wide, profound, complicated and long-lasting impacts on economic and social development in China. Therefore, further measures must be taken in terms of public spending, service supply, infrastructure and elderly care model reform. First, more funding should be channeled to the elderly population to meet their day-to-day consumption needs and to purchase care services; second, the supply of medical care and life care should be increased; third, special attention should be given to build infrastructure, including housing and transport, that are adapted to the needs of the elderly; fourth, society should adapt to the changes in generational relations caused by a reduced family size, and more responsibility should be taken by society as a whole.

3. Building an elderly care system compatible with national conditions

China is providing elderly care to its people at a time when the economy remains underdeveloped. That means the elderly care system should provide what it is required within the boundaries of its capacities. "A sustainable approach must be taken to review the reforms in the elderly care system in China by combining the trends of an ageing population and prospects for economic growth. An elderly care system consistent with China's national conditions must feature both fairness and efficiency."[17] The third plenary session of the 18th central committee of the CPC made it clear that building an elderly care system with Chinese features is one of the key targets of the most recent round of reforms in social security. It demands a proactive response to population ageing, a well-designed policy framework to provide elderly care consistent with China's national conditions, a sound social service system and an elderly service industry. In undertaking these missions, a fairer and more sustainable elderly care system is the key.

VI. Measures to Build a Fairer and More Sustainable Social Security System in China

The report of the 18th National Congress of the CPC stated that the general guideline for social security in China is to provide wide and sustainable coverage to meet basic needs with multiple levels. Institutional fairness requires a wide coverage of all citizens to avoid gaps among regions and industries and between rural and urban areas. Social security should be in line with the nation's economic and social development and the capacity of the public

---

[17] Zhang Monan. *Building an Elderly Care System with Multiple Pillars* [N] China Stocks Paper, February 6, 2012

financial system. Enterprises or state-sponsored institutions are encouraged to set up annuities or pension funds to provide their employees with better retirement plans and employees are advised to purchase commercial insurance plans. A sustainable social security system means that pension funds should be sufficiently financed to secure long-term and stable running of the system.

The *Decision of the Central Committee of the CPC on Some Major Issues Concerning Comprehensively Deepening the Reform* adopted at the third plenary session of the 18th Central Committee of the CPC, which serves as the top-level design blueprint in China, further demands a fairer and more sustainable social security system. The following section explains what it means by 'fairer and more sustainable'.

1. A fairer system secures the rights and interests of participants by putting in place a national pension national security package that features institutional fairness, among industries and regions, and between urban and rural areas.

(1) An incentives institution should provide basic coverage to every citizen and ensure that the more you pay, the more you gain. Pensioners draw their pensions both from individual accounts and the pension national security package. First, basic needs are secured by a basic pension that covers every citizen in society. China first established social insurance systems in state-owned enterprises, which were funded by enterprises under the planned economy system. Gradually, as state-owned enterprises underwent reform, basic social security was established to meet the needs under a market economy. As demanded by a fair and efficient system, an incentive mechanism was established to ensure that the more you pay to the national security package, the more you can draw as your pension. This is another basic principle for elderly care reform that embodies the true meaning of institutional justice.

(2) To reduce the gap between enterprise employees and civil servants in terms of payments and benefits and at the same time improve the reform of the elderly care insurance system for employees of government departments and state-sponsored institutions. The final target is to include enterprise employees and civil servants in one elderly care insurance system to reduce social unfairness. "For the time being, retirees of government departments and state-sponsored institutions draw their pensions according to a certain proportion of their in-service salary, and their pensions are increased as their in-

service colleagues receive a salary increase. Most of the retirees receive more than 70%, while those with senior professional titles receive more than 80%."[18] However, retirees from enterprises receive only 45%. The National School of Development of Peking University believes that average retirees of government departments and state-sponsored institutions receive Rmb24,000 a year, while the corresponding figure for enterprise retirees is Rmb18,000, according to its recently released *Tracking Survey on Health and Elderly Care in China*. To achieve fairness in this regard, the state is boosting reforms to include both enterprise employees and civil servants in the same basic elderly care insurance system that requires civil servants to follow the model of enterprise employees that the employer and employee pay according to laws and regulations. In the meantime, state-sponsored institutions are required to "provide annuities to ensure that retirees will not receive a lower pension to help improve reforms in the elderly care system of civil servants."[19] The ultimate goal is to ensure fairness.

(3) In order to improve fairness among regions, an improvement is needed to transfer payments and policy streamlining among regions, include urban and rural residents in the same basic elderly care insurance system by achieving a smooth transition, secure the current payment base and attract more funding. The elderly care security system in different provinces is established by provincial governments according to local economic and social development levels. As development is imbalanced among provinces and even cities in the same province, elderly care standards differ significantly. This means that cross-region transfer payment becomes difficult, and that between rural and urban systems is even more burdensome. Jin Weigang, director of the social security department at the Ministry of Human Resources and Social Security, says that the "transfer of social security subscriptions can be divided into transfer among regions and that among systems, such as between the rural and urban system; China has 260m migrant workers, of whom 150m migrate between urban and rural areas, and more than 60m across provinces."[20] As long as they leave their homes, the need to transfer subscription arises. Therefore, the key to reform is to find

---

[18] Xu Bo, Zhou Rui. *Top Design is Needed for Elderly Care Insurance Reform* [N] Xinhua Online, August 6, 2013

[19] Xu Bo, Zhou Rui. *Top Design is Needed for Elderly Care Insurance Reform* [N] Xinhua Online, August 6, 2013

[20] Jin Weigang, Bai Tianyao, Li Gang, Cao Lingjuan. *Why 30m Participants Stop Paying for Elderly Care Insurance Every Year* [N] People's Daily, December 10, 2013

a solution for migrant workers. In the past, after withdrawing from an insurance scheme, one was allowed to have the surrendered value refunded into personal accounts. Yet new regulations prohibit the withdrawal and direct drawings of deposit, and because of difficulties associated with cross-region transfer, migrants are unable to continue paying for their insurance in a new area. Nearly half of all provinces are unable to achieve unified fund management at the provincial level, not to mention cross-province transfer. Most of these provinces are located in western areas where the local economy remains underdeveloped. Jin Weigang adds: "In 2012, the surplus in the elderly care fund totaled Rmb2,400bn, but half of that is registered in eastern areas. Many central and western provinces registered deficits and rely on transfer payments from the central government."[21] Developed provinces are therefore cool on the idea of a national security package as they are bound to pay for it, while underdeveloped provinces are also in need of incentives to boost payments and measures to avoid simply relying on central government funds.

The *Social Insurance Law of the PRC* states: "The basic old-age insurance relationship of a member who has worked across different pooling districts shall transfer together with the member, and the member's lengths of contribution payment shall be cumulative. When the member reaches the legal retirement age, his or her basic old-age pension shall be calculated in segregation corresponding to the phases of contribution payment, yet the pension shall be paid in integration as an aggregate. The concrete approach shall be regulated by the State Council." It goes on: "The state shall establish and improve the social insurance of old-age pensions for urban residents. The people's government of a province, autonomous region or municipality directly under the central government may, in accordance with its circumstances, adopt an integrated program to combine its social insurance of the old-age pension for urban residents with its new rural social insurance of the old-age pension."

There's still a long way to go to implement these articles. The next step of reform will unify among regions the rate of payment of individuals and enterprises, the rate of individual contributions, and methods to draw the basic pension. Then, a unified national elderly care insurance system will be established, for all citizens "to ensure reforms are in line with the

---

[21] Jin Weigang, Liu Ling, Liu Mingxia. *Elderly Care Reforms after the Third Plenary Session* [N] Finance National Weekly, December 20, 2013

original intentions".[22] In other words, the key is to achieve nationally unified standards and transfer payments among regions and between rural and urban areas.

2. A sustainable system is built by managing pension funds, putting forward delayed retirement policies and building a system that provides multi-level services.

(1) **Improving the input and management system of pension funds means increasing government inputs and diversifying pension fund investments** First, the government input mechanism must be improved and the budgeting system enhanced. The state should take ultimate responsibility in terms of social basic elderly care insurance. It must take measures to ensure the elderly can draw their basic pension. Government-backed basic insurance also provides allowances to the elderly and those in economic difficulty. It is also responsible for paying the minimum living expenses system. As the government shoulders essential responsibilities in providing social security, the *Decision of the Central Committee of the CPC on Some Major Issues Concerning Comprehensively Deepening the Reform Adopted at the Third Plenary Session of the 18th Central Committee of the CPC* demands to "transfer part of the state-owned capital to social security funds, improve the budgeting system for the operation of state-owned capital, and increase the proportion of state-owned capital gains that are turned over to the public finance to 30% by 2020, to be used to ensure and improve people's livelihoods."[23] Second, to allow diversified investment by pension funds after enhancing management and supervision to improve market-oriented reforms and diversified investment. Allow local pension funds to investment in capital markets in a step-by-step manner to maintain and increase the value of the fund. This is consistent with the general economic trend and internationally agreed practice. While allowing local funds to invest, the principle of long-term, value-oriented and responsible investment must be upheld. The total percentage of investment should be lower than the 40% required for the national fund and 25% for commercial insurance. Portfolio diversification, trusted investment consistent with market practices and supervision according to laws and regulations

---

[22] *More funding is Needed for Elderly Care* [N] China Economy Weekly, October 15, 2012
[23] *Decision of the Central Committee of the CPC on Some Major Issues Concerning Comprehensively Deepening the Reform Adopted at the Third Plenary Session of the 18th Central Committee of the CPC*, November 11, 2013

must be underscored.[24] Zheng Binwen from the China Academy of Social Sciences believes that pension investment should prioritize the preservation and increase in values. In order to achieve higher rates of return, investing in more risky products must be allowed, thus requiring diversified portfolio management. He suggests investment in programs such as high-speed railways to supplement investment in stock markets. Besides, expanding the channels of funding is essential for pension funds, including exploring opportunities in bonds and sovereign wealth funds. The aim is to reduce risks and increase the scale of the fund.

(2) **Develop a gradually delayed retirement policy to expand the pension fund pool** The third plenary session's decision to formulate policies to delay the retirement threshold was the first time that this proposal was written into a formal CPC document. There were two reasons for the timing: (1) the Chinese population is ageing – China now has more than 180m people aged 60 and over, with an annual increase of 5m-8m; (2) there is a deficit in the pension fund pool that requires people to work longer. Despite hot discussion on the matter, postponed retirement will become the only choice as society ages even faster and life expectancy grows, leading to a sharp increase in the number of pension drawers, as well as the number of years that they will benefit from the system. The current retirement policy was introduced in 1951, and many people actually retired much younger than the legal age; the average age is 53. About 20% of the retirees are re-employed, reducing the number of posts released. Hu Xiaoyi, deputy minister of the Ministry of Human Resources and Social Society, says that the policy will be designed in three stages: (1) notice period with an advance; (2) a step-by-step operation, starting from the group with the lowest legal retirement age; (3) a salami tactic that means the retirement threshold will only be delayed by months every year. The authors believe that postponed retirement can increase job supply, expand the pension fund pool and reduce expenditure.

(3) **Building up a multi-level security network that is supported by preferential policies, such as tax waiver and delayed taxation, and encouraging the development of enterprise annuities, professional pension funds and commercial insurance** The traditional Chinese culture and the modern social security mechanism are the two defining factors for China to put in place a diversified and multi-level elderly care

---

[24] Dai Xianglong. *Phrasal Investment of Elderly Care Capital in the Securities Market Recommended* [N] China Securities Online, November 1, 2012

system. "China's population structure is rapidly changing, compounded by the reduced family capacity to take care of the elderly and increased pressure on public spending. A model that includes both government service and socially supported elderly care is the best choice that fits the needs of Chinese society."[25]

A. Underscoring social aid and family-supported elderly care

Social aid provided to people in extreme economic difficulty will continue to be a key area in elderly care. The state will encourage good virtue in families and boost family-supported elderly care. Providing for one's parents is a kind of reciprocity, as everyone will get old. Children will follow the example set by their parents. In the meantime, all kinds of family-based elderly care service must be promoted. A best practice is the community- and family-based elderly care service known as the Golden Sunsets project carried out by the government of Pudong New Area, Shanghai. The government purchased services from social workers to leverage their professional methods and ideas to provide people-oriented, personalized and diverse services. Professionals visit the elderly in their homes or take them to day-time care centers to take care of their everyday needs, offer rehabilitation training services and psychological consultation.[26] Jinyang community in Shanghai is another example. The government there has built roads adapted to the special needs of the elderly, a move that is widely appreciated by senior citizens living in the area.

B. Enhancing support to basic elderly care and encouraging enterprise annuities

Increase the coverage of basic elderly care insurance by providing government subsidies to enterprises and individual payments. More publicity will attract more participants and raise public awareness. The government will design preferential policies to encourage more companies to create enterprise annuities for their employees, which will be funded largely by the enterprise with supplementary payment by the individuals. In the meantime, the Ministry of Human Resources and Social Security and the Ministry of Civil Affairs jointly made announcements that recommend creating enterprise annuities to social organizations and foundations. The announcements also demanded that the total contribution to the annuity generally shall not

---

[25] Zhang Rongnan, *Establishing a Multi-pillared Elderly Care System* [N] China Securities Newspaper, February 6, 2012
[26] Wang Ruihong. *Selected Social Work Projects* [M] East China University of Science and Technology Press, 2010, page 63

exceed one-sixth of an organization's total payroll in the last year. The aim of enterprise annuities is to provide a better guarantee for the payer's retirement.

C. Developing commercial life insurance to boost more types of insurance policies

Buying commercial life insurance must be voluntary. The state will allow high income earners to purchase commercial life insurance to cover their needs to higher-than-basic elderly care services. And more types of insurance policy will be allowed – for instance, tax-deferred elderly care insurance that was first introduced in Shanghai in 2012. This type of insurance allows the policy holder to deduct the insurance premium paid from his taxable income for personal income tax and pay his tax in the future when he draws his pension from the insurer. The reason to encourage commercial life insurance is because pension funds currently register heavy deficits and usually people have only basic social elderly care insurance, although the system is designed to be supported by three pillars: basic social insurance, enterprise and professional annuities, and commercial insurance. The central government issued *Announcement on Issues Concerning Personal Income Tax Calculation of Enterprise and Professional Annuities*, providing that "pursuant to relating regulations of the state, according to the required procedures and under the designated standards, companies' payment to enterprise and professional annuities on behalf of their employers, when added to the employer's personal account, enjoys a waiver of personal income tax, until further notice of the government". The creation of tax-deferred elderly care insurance and the reforms on personal income tax already mentioned are all signs of accelerated and enhanced efforts by the Chinese government to improve the multi-level elderly care service system.

Chapter 8

China's Reform of the Housing Security and Social Relief Systems

In the *Decision of the Central Committee of the CPC on Some Major Issues Concerning Comprehensively Deepening Reform* adopted at the third plenary session of the 18th Central Committee of the CPC in 2013, the CPC stated: "In order to make sure that more fruits of development are shared by all the people in a fair way, we must accelerate the reform of social undertakings, satisfactorily resolve the most pressing and real problems of the greatest concern to the people, and better satisfy people's demands." Housing and social relief are pillars of the social security system and play a positive role in ensuring social harmony and stability. This chapter will analyze China's housing security reform background and measures, as well as that of the social relief system, introduce the system of publicly accumulated housing funds, the system of generally affordable and functional housing, the low-rent housing system, and the public housing rental program. China's social relief system is also introduced. In conclusion, this chapter also discusses poverty alleviation policies in China.

I. China's Multi-level Housing Security System

The multi-level housing security system aims to secure the right to housing of low-to-medium income earners by taking multi-level and diverse measures. The system is mainly supported by the government, market and social organizations through compulsory policies or collaborative programs.[27]

China's current measures to address housing security are to build up a multi-level housing security system. The country is in urgent need of a system that can adhere to the diversified needs of different communities, including

---

[27] Dong Jiayan. *Research on Multi-layer Housing Security in China's Urban Areas* [D] Shandong Economics University, 2011

underprivileged families, introduced talent and urban professionals. It is designed according to the following factors: (1) income; (2) past experience; (3) family housing conditions; (4) household economic difficulty. The government provides subsidies according to these factors to help those in need. By introducing different policies, the state strives to secure, as much as possible, the highest degree of social fairness.

Having evolved for more than four decades, China now has four systems to secure housing for its people under the guideline of providing targeted support to families with different levels of income.

1. The system of publicly accumulated housing funds

All levels of state departments, state-sponsored institutions, state-owned enterprises, urban collectively owned companies, foreign-funded companies and private enterprise are required by law to pay an employee monthly fee, supplemented by an employee's personal payment, which will be deposited long term to provide for the purchase, building and renovation of housing of the employee's family.

Shanghai was the first city in China to create pilot programs of publicly accumulated housing funds in 1991, aimed at creating a government-backed financing channel for urban working families. Based on the experience gained in Shanghai, the Ministry of Finance, Leading Group of the State Council on Housing Reform and the People's Bank of China jointly issued *Interim Rules on Establishing Publicly Accumulated Housing Funds* to start national implementation of the policy. In order to further strengthen and regulate management of publicly accumulated housing funds, the State Council published *Management Regulations on Publicly Accumulated Housing Funds* in April 1999, followed by amendments in 2002 that serve as guidelines for the funds.

By the end of 2010, the Ministry of Housing and Urban and Rural Construction issued *Announcement to Adjust Deposit and Lending Interest Rates of Publicly Accumulated Housing Funds* that allowed the funds to provide loans to government-subsidized housing projects to promote the development of this type of housing.

As a kind of government-backed and policy-guaranteed solidarity fund, the publicly accumulated housing funds are conducive to raising funds for housing construction and helping people purchase commercial houses. To date, most cities in China have separate institutions (management centers) to manage publicly accumulated housing funds, and management committees are set up to take decisions regarding the running of funds. Government finance department supervision and the system of depositing the funds in a specially appointed bank account are established to ensure fund safety. These are helpful to accumulate funds for house-building projects, promote government-sponsored housing projects and provide housing for low-to-middle-income households.

2. The system of generally affordable and functional housing

This system provides social welfare commercial houses to low-to-middle-income households that are priced below market level thanks to preferential policies from the government that allow property developers to acquire cheaper land and pay lower administrative fees and tax. The government also requires developers to build this kind of property according to a set of criteria and sell the houses to qualified customers with a limited profit. It regulates that these houses are usually around 60-80 square meters to meet the needs of average families so that more people can benefit.

The State Council promulgated *Decision on Deepening Reforms in the Urban Housing System* and *Regulations on the Management of Generally Affordable and Functional Housing*, in which these houses are required to be targeted at urban low-to-middle-income households and are economical, practical and serving social security needs. After 1998, the state stopped providing in-kind houses to qualified citizens, a program known as '*anju*' (living happily), and started to support the construction of commercially sold, generally affordable and functional houses.

Supplying generally affordable and functional houses contributes to keeping property prices in a reasonable range by increasing aggregate market supply, especially of average houses. It also helps some low-to-middle-income households ensure their housing rights, and has become an important part of the housing security system.

3. The low-rent housing system

Low-rent housing, also known as public housing, refers to the average houses provided by the government to families with the lowest income who have urban household registration certificates or other families that need help from the social welfare system. It is an act of the state to perform its social welfare role. The government either requires the family to pay rent that is lower than the market price, or offers cash subsidies to qualified families to rent average houses from the market.

All levels of governments in China started this system in 1998. The Ministry of Construction issued its No. 70 decree to promulgate *Regulations on the Urban Low-Rent Housing System*. In March 2004, the Ministry of Construction, Ministry of Finance, Ministry of Land and Resources, and State Administration of Taxation jointly published decree No. 120 to put into effect *Regulations on the Urban Low-Rent Housing System for Families with the Lowest Incomes*. These rules and regulations established a legal framework for the low-rent housing system.

4. The system of public housing rental program

China has yet to enact a policy regarding public housing rental programs at the national level, while many cities are carrying out meaningful experiments. This system is aimed at providing a solution to the 'sandwich class' housing problem, including migrant workers, university graduates and a new generation of urban citizens. As urbanization accelerates, property prices rise. The 'sandwich class' cannot afford commercial houses, and are qualified for existing welfare housing. Their living conditions are poor, and are compared to ants and snails. The public housing rental program system is therefore designed to meet their needs.

In Chongqing city alone, more than 300,000 square meters of collective dormitories or apartments were supplied by renovating empty houses and unused factory buildings in 2008. By the end of that year, 810,000 square meters of affordable housing were provided to migrant workers in Chongqing. Another 250,000 square meters were added in the first half of 2009. Then Chongqing mayor Huang Qibao believes that rental housing not only helps the 'sandwich class' people, but also can be rented to low-income households or to households with special needs after receiving a subsidy from the government.[28]

A number of governments actively followed the practice of Chongqing, and vigorously developed public rental housing construction with good results. In Qingdao, for example, almost all households with housing difficulties can find a solution from the housing security system. After years of effort, the government of Qingdao designed a network of housing security and supply with four basic systems and two supplementary channels – low-rent housing, generally affordable and functional housing, commercial housing with price ceilings, government-invested rental housing and rental housing funded by developers. At the moment, the government is looking into the feasibility of combining the low-rent housing system and the government-subsidized rental housing system in a bid to cover more 'sandwich class' families.[29]

Compared with generally affordable and functional housing and low-rent housing, public rental houses feature low rent, a stable relationship with the landowner and help with educating people to develop a healthy housing consumption pattern. The state was determined to make this system a pillar of the housing security system in 2011-2015. This is a meaningful experiment of the Chinese government to respond to the accelerated trend of urbanization and industrialization, as well as provide equal services to both urban and rural areas.

II. China's Social Relief System

In order to help the lives of urban families with low incomes or those facing economic difficulty, China started to put in place a guarantee system of a minimum standard of living for urban residents in 1994. This marked the introduction of the social relief system, followed by a wider range coverage in rural areas.

1. Guarantee system of minimum standard of living for urban residents

This is a new type of social relief system aimed at improving the traditional

---

[28] Liu Jian. Xu Xuzhong. *Dual Track Housing System: Allowing Low- and Medium-income People Choose Where to Live* [N] International Financing Daily, October 25, 2010
[29] Tong Yidi. *Housing Security: Practice in Some Cities* [J] Housing Industry, 2009 (10) 60-63

system that lacks a unified and reasonable criteria set. Implementation of the system in many cities has proved that a guarantee system of a minimum standard of living for urban residents can improve the effectiveness and efficiency of relief work, ensuring fairness and accuracy in finding those in need, securing a reasonable level of social relief and making social relief work more standard-based, institutionalized and legally administered.

In 1993, Shanghai became the first city in the country to establish a guarantee system of a minimum standard of living for urban residents. The system, also known as minimum living cost guarantee level for urban residents, was created by the state to help those urban residents whose income is insufficient to cover basic living costs. A threshold line for the system is its unique feature that distinguishes it from old-style social relief systems.

The Ministry of Civil Affairs praised the practices in Shanghai and proposed the national implementation of the system in 1994. In 1996, the state published the *Ninth Five-year Plan on National Economic and Social Development and Framework Long-term Targets for 2010* that advocated "the establishment of a guarantee system of minimum standard of living for urban residents". In September 1997, the State Council issued the *Announcement to Establish a Guarantee System of Minimum Standard of Living for Urban Residents in All Cities*.

By the end of 1999, the system was established in most cities. By the end of 2002, all citizens who had met the requirements were given government subsidies under the system, which are adjusted frequently. By the end of 2003, a law, rules and a regulations system were set up and agencies to govern and run the system were established. This system effectively secured the basic needs of low-income urban communities, including laid-off employees of state-owned enterprises. It helped to uphold economic structural reforms, social stability and harmony, as well as the coordinated development of society and the economy.

2. Guarantee system of minimum standard of living for rural residents

Institutional help given to people in extreme economic difficulty in rural areas of Shanghai municipality was pioneered in the 1990s with pilot programs in Shanghai and Yangquan, Shanxi province. The Ministry of Civil Affairs decided to "establish basic-level social security systems in rural areas with different thresholds and standards that are consistent with local economic development" at the 10th national working conference on civil affairs held in 1994.[30] By the end of 2001, 2,037 counties (cities and city districts) in 21 provinces (autonomous regions and municipalities directly under the jurisdiction of the central government) established a guarantee system of a minimum standard of living for rural residents, covering 3.44m people. In 2007, the State Council issued *Announcement to Establish a Guarantee System of a Minimum Standard of Living for Rural Residents in China* that demanded national implementation, according to which local governments stepped up their efforts in this area.

In 1994, the State Council issued *Regulations on the Work of Providing Five Guarantees in Rural Areas*, requiring local governments to set up institutional and standardized systems to help people without family support and who are unable to secure regular income. By the end of 2008, this social relief scheme covered more than 5.4m people, covering basically everyone in need.

The Chinese government believes that it should provide help to all people that meet the requirements. Minimum living cost standards differ from region to region and in rural and urban areas as economic imbalances prevail. For example, by the end of June 2012, 533,700 people in Chongqing municipality received an urban minimum living cost subsidy and 833,500 received a rural subsidy. The municipality is divided into three areas: (1) Level A areas in which urban residents received a monthly subsidy of Rmb320, and rural residents Rmb170; (2) Level B areas, where urban residents received Rmb305, and rural residents received Rmb160; (3) Level C areas, where urban residents received Rmb290; and rural residents received Rmb150.[31]

> **Example:**
> **May 12, 2008, Wenchuan Earthquake Relief**
>
> An earthquake broke out at 2.28pm on May 12, 2008 that caused unprecedented damage and casualties. Relief work was carried out despite huge difficulties under the care and strong leadership of the CPC Central Committee and State Council, whose directions gave clear instruction on the work that served as a basic guarantee for successful and proactive relief work.
>
> One was to organize rescue personnel. In earthquake relief work, the government had always adhered to the people-oriented principle to take saving

---

[30] Zhang Haiyin, Tang Jun, editor. *A Dictionary on Social Securities* [M] Beijing: Economy Management Press, 1993: 234
[31] *Chongqing to Revise Minimum Living Wage*, Chongqing Business Daily, [N] July 24, 2012

people's lives as the primary task. Rescue personnel were racing against time to help the wounded and find the trapped. A total of 140,000 People's Liberation Army servicemen, armed police, fire-fighters, policemen, militia members and reserve forces personnel, along with 48,680 medical emergency staff, rushed to the affected areas. A total of 83,988 people were rescued from the rubble.

Two was to actively raise money for disaster relief. Sichuan provincial finance department received a special fund of Rmb5.386bn for earthquake relief, of which the central government appropriated Rmb4.083bn. Provincial and municipal (state) financial departments allocated relief funds totaling Rmb5.632bn, of which provincial funds totaled Rmb4.1bn and municipal-level funds totaled Rmb1.532bn. According to incomplete statistics, Sichuan province received a total of Rmb2.833bn-worth of donations. After the disaster, market supplies were quickly restored and prices stabilized.

Three was stepping up repair work to damaged infrastructure as soon as possible to guarantee communication, electricity and water so as to create conditions for earthquake relief, which was a pressing matter immediately after the quake. Major motorways leading to affected areas, including Beichuan, Qingchuan, Pingwu, Mao, Li and Wenchuan, were restored shortly after the disaster. Traffic was stopped on 33 roads. All 109 villages and towns in eight counties that were cut off from communication networks were re-connected. The earthquake shut down power supply to 1,307 townships and counties, of which 1,203 were restored. Out of 10,457 villages with no energy, 10,028 had been reconnected with emergency power. Efforts were stepped up to repair damaged water supply infrastructure, and relief workers brought water tanks to guarantee basic water supplies. Water conservation projects were given special attention by strengthening monitoring over reservoirs and quake-affected lakes. Emergency plans were put in place.

Four was to strive for the resettlement of affected people. As far as possible, the affected people were transferred to safer places. Victim relief stations were set up, providing food, drinking water, tents and other basic necessities to ensure the affected people had food to eat and clean water to drink, clothes to wear and a temporary place to live. The State Council subsidized each affected person with Rmb10 in cash and 1kg of grain. It also provided orphans, along with the elderly with no children and the disabled with no family members, a subsidy of Rmb600 yuan per month. The government carried out identity checks to find out the beneficiaries.

Five was to have comprehensive disease control and prevention in the affected areas. The prevention of major epidemics after the disaster was an important part of the earthquake relief work. Early prevention, early deployment and early preparation were underscored. Six million copies of *Unified Manual on On-site Health and Disease Control Works after an Earthquake* were distributed. A total of 9,543 health workers were dispatched, and 19.2m tons of medicine were dispensed and 429m square meters of land sterilized. Some 3,450 health inspection officers were sent to monitor water quality, and gave advice on water usage to the affected. Measures were immediately taken to cover the bodies of victims, and 50,766 bodies were cremated or buried.

Six was to effectively safeguard social stability in the disaster area. Security patrols were strengthened to prevent theft, robbery and other crimes; emphasis was placed on strengthening the security of banks, shops, etc. The radio, television, the internet and mobile phone text messages were used to strengthen public opinion guidance and to conduct propaganda and mobilization to prevent the spread of rumors and quell public panic. The monitoring and forecasting of aftershocks were strengthened and the latest information was released in a timely manner. By May 22, 2008, Sichuan Provincial People's Government Information Office held 10 press conferences in Chengdu. All levels of CPC organizations organized official and youth volunteers to comfort the affected, in particular bereaved families. The affected areas remained stable.

3. Medical aid system

Since the mid-1990s, China has carried out a fundamental reform of the whole social security system, making it consistent with the establishment and improvement of a socialist market economy. It has also paid more attention to social security in the realization of social and economic coordination. China started pilot programs in some counties, cities and city districts where local regulations and detailed rules were formulated and implemented. Urban and rural medical aid is important to help people in extreme economic difficulty to access medical care. At the moment, China's medical aid system is mainly composed of social medical insurance, a new type of cooperative medical insurance and an urban and rural medical aid system. The latter acts as supplement to the first two.

In November 2003, according to the CPC Central Committee and the State Council's *Decision to Further Enhance Medical Services in Rural Areas*, the Ministry of Civil Affairs, in conjunction with the Ministry of Finance and the Ministry of Health, issued *Opinions on Implementing Medical Aid Funds in Rural Areas*. The Ministry of Finance and the Ministry of Civil Affairs jointly issued *Regulations on the Management of Medical Aid Funds in Rural Areas* that improved the rural medical aid system. In March 2005, the State Council clarified the role of the Ministry of Civil Affairs, Ministry of Health, Ministry of Labor and Social Security, and Ministry of Finance in the coordination of urban and rural area development, as well as regional coordination and other areas involved in building a harmonious society. It believes that social relief is the focus of the entire social security reform. By the end of 2008, all capital towns of cities, districts and counties were covered by the urban medical aid system and the rural medical aid system was implemented in all rural areas.

4. The relief system for the homeless and beggars

In order to provide further help for people with economic difficulties in urban and rural areas, in recent years, the Ministry of Civil Affairs, in cooperation with other authorities, issued *Announcements on Further Improving Education and Aid to Minors with Special Difficulties*, *Regulations on the Management of Providing Low-Rent Housing to Households with the Lowest Income in Urban Areas*, and *Opinions on Implementing the Regulations on Legal Aid and Helping Citizens with Economic Difficulties to Access Judiciary Services*, providing fundamental institutional design for educational aid, housing aid, legal and judiciary aid in both rural and urban areas. All levels of government attach importance to helping the homeless and beggars. In August 2003, the State Council adopted *Regulations on Managing Aid to the Homeless and Beggars in Cities*, demanding a paradigm shift from the compulsory detention and sending back of such people to their address registered with the police department, to active help and emphasizing voluntary acceptance of aid. In January 2006, the General Office of the State Council, in its *Opinions on Legislation Work of the State Council in 2006*, requested the Ministry of Civil Affairs to draft the *Law on Social Relief*, which marked the start of the legislation process.

5. China's policy to improve the multi-level social relief system

(1) Transforming from a government-monopolized system to one that involves government, enterprises and civil society organizations

Social relief work in China has long been the responsibility of governments in urban areas and collectively owned economic units, such as villages in rural areas. Despite the willingness of other enterprises, social organizations and ordinary citizens to participate, they are not capable of doing so. In a market economy, the state remains the principal and only provider of social relief, but the resources needed are jointly supplied by volunteer organizations, companies and other social organizations.

The government's role in social relief will improve. At present, China's social relief system is in transition. The government is unable to do everything and social organizations are not well developed to help out. One way out is an improved institutionalized and standardized social relief system, which means injecting more rule of law in this aspect by promoting the development of a charity market and raising people's awareness. It also needs to improve the mechanism to allow more volunteer work, cultivate a market for philanthropic activities, enhance the capacity building of non-governmental organizations, and encourage enterprises to honor their social obligations and responsibilities.[32]

The government's primary responsibilities are formulating laws and regulations to supervise and manage social relief work accordingly. It needs to promote fund-raising activities that are lawful, and safeguard the lawful rights of charities, donors and beneficiaries. At present, the government plays the role of money-raiser and supervisor at the same time. It should fully encourage charity organizations to take the initiative within the legal framework, stop raising money directly and only play an active role as supervisor. It also should fully mobilize various resources. Information technology should be fully leveraged, and an e-government framework should be put in place to manage donations. And various volunteer activities should be promoted. In this way, the government will be more efficient in administrative work, reduce costs and fully attract social capital to play a major role in charity.

Therefore, it is imperative for the government to design aid platforms, relief mechanisms and guidance manuals to better administer social relief activities. It also needs to mobilize, encourage and attract all kinds of social charity organizations, aid funds and non-governmental organizations to provide more help and services to those in need.

A full role in social relief will be given to social organizations. They are effective bridges connecting donors and aid providers. They can fully mobilize social resources to raise funds and take money and material resources to those most in need in a timely manner so that their problems can be alleviated and

---

[32] Zhu Yinduan, Zhuang Xifu. *Brief Discussion on the Scientific Development Outlook and Social Securities* [J] Scientific Socialism, 2009 (3):100-103

they will recognize the generosity of society and therefore seek to actively do some good things in return.

Social organizations have various functions to perform in social relief. (1) Make publicity to encourage more donations. Social organizations therefore need to reach out actively to promote high quality projects so that companies and society members will know better what charity means to the advancement of society and the development of their businesses, which will lead to more self-motivated charity activities. That will, in turn, lead to better development of charity in China. (2) Provide social relief in an accurate and timely manner. Social organizations should strive to choose the most efficient and effective way to help so that they can achieve best results. Organizations must respect the intentions of donors, carry out due investigation to understand the needs of vulnerable groups and then contact related parties to ensure that money is spent in the most appropriate places, therefore enhancing social justice and fairness. The beneficiaries can also recognize kindness and care from their peers. (3) Manage and use donations in an open and transparent manner. People's trust and participation in social relief work will be enhanced as a consequence, and donations can be used more effectively. Social organizations must ensure the safety of donations and that they are being spent on projects identified by donors.

(2) Transforming from purely providing aid to guaranteeing life standards and helping the needy to become independent

The ultimate goal of social relief is to help vulnerable people help themselves and become self-reliant, and consequently able to help others in return. It is the primary responsibility of the social relief system to ensure basic living needs, which also includes psychological needs to live a decent life and be respected. Therefore, a new type of social relief system must aim at realizing the full positional of those in need, help them adapt to society, and lead a life that they can feel satisfied with. In implementing social relief, welfare dependency must be avoided. The system must make sure that subsidies only play a role in supplementing the gap between what the beneficiaries earn from working and what they need for basic life. In other words, applicants must make every effort to make a living, either depending on their own capital, abilities or other resources. Only hard-working applicants can qualify for social relief if they still can't maintain a basic life.[33]

---

[33] Zhu Xunke. *Research on Relief System in Modern Society and its Transformational Justice* [J] China Civil Affairs, 2008 (4) 24-26

(3) Establishing a day-to-day working mechanism for donations and improving supervision on social relief

This mechanism will create a standardized and institutionalized donation channel that runs on a regular basis, which will allow more aid activity, including mutual help and assistance that will attract more funds to be invested into social relief work, supplementing government input. Social relief, therefore, can provide more help to those in need, and make their lives better.

In the meantime, the supervision mechanism over social relief work must be improved to exercise rule-based and effective supervision. Media, all levels of people's congresses and CPPCC committees, all sorts of governmental institutions, the CPC, democratic parties, relevant social organizations, civil society organizations, and especially the masses, should be involved in the supervision of social relief institutions, professionals, funds and in-kind resources to ensure an effective and fair service.

III. China's Poverty-alleviation Policy

Since the reform and opening up, the Chinese government's poverty-alleviation policy has experienced four stages. First stage: 1978-1985. The main feature of this stage was relying on institutional reforms to release productivity, and poverty was reduced thanks to the momentum achieved by the increased working morale of farmers, who were allowed to sign a contract to lease land for their families. They were no longer required to submit all production to the state and, instead, permission was given to those who completed tasks regulated by the contracts. In the meantime, agricultural produce prices were raised to increase farmers' incomes and create better conditions for related transactions. The per capita net income of farmers increased by 16.5% annually, and poverty numbers were halved from 250m in 1985 to 125m in 1978. The poverty rate fell from 33.1% in the early days of the reforms to 14.8% in 1985.

Second stage: 1986-1993. After further reform measures were introduced to improve the market economy in the mid-1980s, growth rate gaps started to widen between the agricultural and industrial sectors, rural and urban areas, and among regions. At the same time, the poverty reduction trend slowed down. The Chinese government first implemented targeted policies in the seventh five-year plan by identifying 331 national key counties for poverty alleviation. The state appropriated funds to facilitate development in these areas. In the eighth five-year plan, 236 counties were added to the list. Headway was made after introducing these policies, yet more effort was needed. In 1993, poverty numbers in rural areas were reduced further to 75m, equivalent to 8.2% of total rural population.

Third stage: 1994-2000. In 1994, the Chinese government announced a national plan to alleviate poverty, known as the 'Eight Seven' plan. It declared that it would focus on poverty over the next seven years to reduce poverty numbers by 2000, which at the time stood at 80m. That goal was achieved by the end of 2000 when people living in poverty totaled 30m, accounting for around 3% of the rural population. The implementation of the plan helped key counties grow by an annual rate of 7.5% in the agriculture sector, 12% in industry, 12.9% in public revenue and 12.8% in per capita annual income of farmers.

The fourth stage: 2001-2010. In the 21st century, China's poverty-alleviation and development work entered a new stage. By the end of 2000, 30m were still living under the poverty line and 60m were classified as having low incomes. These 90m people were major targets of China's poverty alleviation work in the new century. They were living in geographically more sporadic areas with even harder natural conditions and lower social development levels, making poverty reduction even more difficult. In May 2001, the Central Committee of the CPC released *Framework Plan on Poverty Reduction and Development in China's Rural Areas (2001-2010)*, which was another guiding document after the 'Eight Seven' Plan.

Chapter 8

The United Nations Development Program believes that China's achievements in poverty alleviation "provide a model for developing countries, and even the entire world". This model features: (1) Development alongside social security and relief. The government helps people and areas stricken by poverty to turn to the market and strengthen their own capacity to self-development. (2) Combining targeted national plans and industrial and social efforts. Special plans on poverty alleviation were made and implemented ever year with government funds as the main source of financing. State water resources and transportation administrations take poverty-stricken areas as their main target of investment. State institutions and private enterprises partner with these areas to help. Cities, counties, even provinces in eastern and western areas pair up to help each other. Army servicemen and armed police forces also take part in the process. Social organizations are involved, too. All measures are aimed at improving development in poverty-stricken areas and giving farmers more income. (3) Combining outside help and local efforts. All measures, including targeted poverty-reduction funds, transfer payments from the central government, department projects, donations and foreign investment are explored to increase funding to these areas, while people living in these areas are also working hard to combat poverty.

Chapter Follow-up Questions and References

Chapter 1

Questions for consideration:

1. How are people's congresses in China elected and how do they operate?
2. What are the institutions at the central level of the CPC?
3. How do China's political consultation conferences operate?
4. Why can't China adopt the separation of three powers like in western countries?
5. What's your opinion of China's grassroots mass autonomy?

References:

1. Pu Zuxing. *On the Political System of China*, [M] Shanghai: Fudan University Press, 2007
2. Li Tianxi. *An Introduction to China's Political Development* [M] Beijing: Intellectual Property Publishing House, 2013
3. Zhou Tianyong, Gong Jian. *Research Report on China's Political System Reform* [M] Xinjiang: Press of Xinjiang Production and Construction Corps, 2008

Chapter 2

Questions for consideration:

1. How is the central government of China organized?
2. What functions does the central government perform?
3. How are China's administrative regions demarcated?
4. How does the system of government in China differ from western developed countries?

References:

1. Chen Yao. *Contemporary China's Government System* [M] Shanghai: Shanghai Jiaotong University Press, 2005
2. Zhang Chengfu. *Social Changes and Government Innovation: 30 Years of China's Government Reform* [M] Beijing: China Renmin University, 2009
3. Shen Ronghua. *China's Government Reform: Major Problems* [M] Beijing: Society Publishing House of China, 2012
4. Guo Liancheng. *Research on Economic Globalization and the Transformation of Government Functions in Transitional Countries.* Beijing: Commercial Press, 2011

Chapter 3

Questions for consideration:

1. How does the Chinese government promote more equal public services?
2. What are the challenges facing developing countries in providing public services and how should they be addressed?

References:

1. Ju Hua. *Market Mechanism in Public Service: Theory, Methodology and Techniques* [M] Beijing: Peking University Press, 2006
2. China (Hainan) Institute for Reform and Development. *Essential Public Service and Human Development in China* [M] Beijing: China Economy Press, 2008
3. Chen Chanshen, Cai Yuezhou. *Government System Changes in the Light of Regional Comprehensive Assessment* [M] Beijing: China Social Science Press, 2007

Chapter 4

Questions for consideration:

1. What has China achieved in CE?
2. What are the policies aimed at achieving education equality?
3. What common challenges face developing countries in achieving education equality?

References:

1. Wu Degang. *Research on China's Compulsory Education* [M] Beijing: Education Science Press, 2011
2. Wu Degang. *Research on China's Education Reform and Development* [M] Beijing: Education Science Press, 2011
3. Ye Lan. *Research on Primary Education Reform and Development* [M] Beijing: China Renmin University Press, 2009
4. Yang Dongping, *Towards 2020: Strategy for China's Education Reform* [M] Beijing: Renmin Press, 2010
5. Yang Dongping, *Dreams and Realities of China's Education Equality* [M] Beijing: Peking University Press, 2007
6. Tan Songhua. *Theory and Practice of China's Education Reform and Development* [J] Education Research, Volume 3, 2003

Chapter 5

Questions for consideration:

1. How has public service in China developed and improved?
2. What are China's best practices and policies in providing public service?

References:

1. *Labor Law of the PRC*, website of the central government of the PRC
2. *Law of the PRC on the Promotion of Small and Medium-sized Enterprises*, website of the central government of the PRC
3. *Trade Union Law of the PRC*, website of the central government of the PRC
4. *Labor Contract Law of the PRC*, website of the central government of the PRC
5. *Employment Promotion Law of the PRC*, website of the central government of the PRC
6. *Social Insurance Law of the PRC*, website of the central government of the PRC
7. *Regulations on Unemployment Insurance*, website of the central government of the PRC
8. *Interim Measures on Collective Bargaining*, website of the central government of the PRC

Chapter Follow-up Questions and References

9. *Provisions on Collective Contracts*, website of the central government of the PRC
10. *Provisions on Minimum Wages*, website of the central government of the PRC
11. *Provisions on Employment Services and Employment Management*, website of the central government of the PRC
12. *China's Employment*, www.lm.gov.cn

Chapter 6

Questions for consideration:

1. What are the basic features of China's current medical care system?
2. Try to divide China's health care reform into stages. How many are there? What are the criteria?
3. What measures have been taken by the Chinese government to ensure universal access to basic public health care?

References:

1. Li Jiuyi. *Guidelines on Grassroots-level Medical and Health Care System Reform and Management* [M] Beijing: People's Daily Press, 2005
2. All-China Federation of Trade Unions. *Compilation of Documents on Medical and Health Care System* [M] Beijing: Worker's Press of China, 2011

Chapter 7

Questions for consideration:

1. The final goal of China's elderly care system reform is to create a uniform standard for the country by transforming and combining local and regional systems. How can it achieve this goal?
2. How can China solve the inadequate funding for pensions and preserve/increase the value of pension funds?
3. Can China delay its retirement threshold? How does it respond to the resultant employment challenges?

References:

1. Tian Baotian et al. *Social Security in China* [M] Beijing: Wuzhou Communications, 2006
2. Wang Xiaozhang. *Social Security in China's Developed Areas* [M] Zhejiang: Zhejiang University Press, 2007

3. Tong Limin. *Social Work for the Elderly* [M] Shanghai: East China University of Science and Technology Press, 2006

4. Wang Ruihong. *Selected Social Work Projects* [M] East China University of Science and Technology Press, 2010, page 63.